VICKI JAMISON PETERSON
GOD'S ANOINTED VESSEL

A Life of Miracles, Healing, and Faith

Dr Michael H Yeager

All rights reserved. No part of this book is allowed to be reproduced, stored in a retrieval system, or transmitted by any form or by any means-electronic, mechanical, photocopy, recording, or otherwise-without prior written permission of the copyright owner, except by a reviewer who wishes to quote brief passages in connection with a review for inclusion in a magazine, website, newspaper, podcast, or broadcast. All Scripture quotations, unless otherwise indicated, are taken from the King James Authorized Version of the Bible.

This book contains information from public sources found online. This book also includes info based on the author's real-life experiences.

Copyright © 2024 Dr Michael H Yeager

All rights reserved.

ISBN: 9798344588728

DEDICATION

To those who yearn, who are genuinely hungry and thirsty to live in the realm of the supernatural, this book is for you. To those who have already tasted the glories of the heavenly realm, this is dedicated to you. To the bride of **Jesus Christ**, who is called to delve deeper, to soar higher, and to journey farther than ever before, this dedication stands as a **Testament**. It is only by the unmerited grace of our Lord, obtained through unwavering FAITH in **JESUS CHRIST**, that we can hope to achieve His divine will on this earth. As we face the adversary, Satan, and the powers of darkness, may we always remember our purpose and calling.

CONTENTS

ACKNOWLEDGMENTS

1	Chapter One	1
2	Chapter Two	18
3	Chapter Three	40
4	Chapter Four	63
5	Chapter Five	85
6	Chapter Six	104
7	Chapter Seven	125
8	Chapter Eight	144
9	Chapter Nine	160
10	Chapter Ten	179

ACKNOWLEDGMENTS
"Vicki Jamison-Peterson: A Life of Faith, Healing, and Transforming Love in Christ"

During her 35 years of ministry, Vicki Jamison-Peterson embodied the power and love of Jesus Christ in everything she did. Her ministry reached across borders and touched lives all around the world, from England to Switzerland, Australia to Germany, and countless places in between. Known as an evangelist and a soul winner, Vicki had a passion for leading others to Jesus. In her New England crusades alone, more than 20,000 souls came to Christ over three years, with churches springing up as a lasting fruit of this revival. In Chicago, her compassion led her to establish "New Day House," a ministry that provided housing and support for unwed mothers and their children—a place of refuge and new beginnings.

Vicki's talents extended beyond preaching; she was also a gifted author, vocalist, and psalmist. Her writings on Christian life included well-loved books like *El Shaddai* (later re-titled *More Than Enough*) and *How You Can Have Joy*, each offering insights into the abundant life God promises.

Vicki's music ministry was equally impactful, with eight albums filled with songs she wrote and recorded. Her voice, both spoken and sung, carried the message of Christ's love. As a pioneer in Christian media, she brought her heart for the gospel to the airwaves, producing two television programs, *It's a New Day* and *Vicki Live*. She appeared regularly on major Christian television networks, sharing the message of hope and healing in Jesus with countless viewers.

Truly, Vicki's ministry was beyond labels. Her influence went

Vicki Jamison Peterson: God's Anointed Vessel

across denominations and broke down barriers of race, gender, and culture. In South Africa, following the end of apartheid, she was the first to hold interracial worship services, uniting believers in the name of Christ. As a trailblazer for women in ministry, Vicki helped open doors, empowering women in the church to embrace their calling boldly.

Through her ministry, God moved powerfully to heal the sick, deliver the oppressed, and bring people from every walk of life face-to-face with the living God. As Vicki often shared, the gospel of Jesus Christ has the power to transform lives: ***"Jesus Christ the same yesterday, and today, and forever"*** (Hebrews 13:8, KJV). With a heart filled with love for the Lord and His people, Vicki Jamison-Peterson left a legacy that continues to inspire, heal, and bring people into a deeper relationship with Jesus.

Dr Michael H Yeager

CHAPTER ONE
"Vicki Jamison Peterson: A Life of Healing, Faith, and Love in Christ"

In the heart of the Charismatic Renewal movement of the 1970s, a powerful figure emerged from Dallas, Texas—Vicki Jamison Peterson. Born in 1936, Vicki grew up with a humble heart but an extraordinary gift. She discovered her calling as a Pentecostal healing evangelist, a role that would lead her into the homes and hearts of thousands across the world. Known for her dynamic preaching and profound ability to minister healing through Jesus Christ, Vicki's services became well-known for miracles, spiritual revival, and the unmistakable presence of God.

Vicki's meetings drew people from all walks of life, each coming with a hunger for hope, healing, and truth. In her powerful gatherings, Vicki invited people to encounter the healing touch of Jesus. Like the multitudes that pressed upon Jesus in the Gospels, these crowds sought her ministry not for spectacle but because they saw the evidence of true healing. Many experienced physical and emotional freedom that doctors and therapists could not provide. In these gatherings, she often referenced verses like **Matthew 11:28**, "Come unto me, all ye that

labour and are heavy laden, and I will give you rest." For Vicki, Jesus' invitation to come was central to her message—He alone could provide the healing balm for every wound, both seen and unseen.

Through her television program, *Vicki Jamison-Peterson Ministries,* her message reached far beyond church walls, entering living rooms around the world. With warmth and humility, Vicki spoke to viewers like friends, using her broadcast to pray for their needs, offer spiritual encouragement, and teach the truth of Jesus' love. Her compassionate approach helped break down barriers, ensuring everyone who watched felt genuinely loved and valued.

Beyond physical healing, Vicki also focused on emotional and inner healing. She understood that many carried invisible wounds—heartbreak, guilt, shame—that hindered them from fully embracing God's love. She would often share how Jesus, described in **Isaiah 53:5** as the one **"wounded for our transgressions,"** came to heal both the body and the soul. Through her teachings, people were able to release their burdens, find inner peace, and walk in newness of life. Vicki was known for saying, **"Jesus loves you as you are, but He loves you too much to leave you that way."**

In addition to her role as an evangelist, Vicki was a gifted singer who often led worship before delivering her sermons. She believed music was a pathway to the heart, allowing the Holy Spirit to move freely among those gathered. Her voice brought a comforting sense of God's presence and prepared hearts for the ministry of healing

Vicki Jamison Peterson: God's Anointed Vessel

that followed. As people sang with her, they could sense God's love washing over them, breaking down walls and setting the stage for miraculous transformations.

Though her ministry saw tremendous success, Vicki faced many personal trials, yet she held tightly to her faith, grounded in the promises of God. She would often remind herself and her audience of verses like **Isaiah 41:10, "Fear thou not; for I am with thee: be not dismayed; for I am thy God: I will strengthen thee; yea, I will help thee; yea, I will uphold thee with the right hand of my righteousness."** Through each difficulty, Vicki chose to rely on the strength of Jesus, encouraging others to do the same.

As her health declined in the early 2000s, Vicki continued to press on, never wavering in her devotion to Christ. By the time she passed in 2008, she had left an indelible mark on countless lives, showing the world that Jesus is both Savior and Healer, Friend and King. Her legacy is one of enduring faith, boundless love, and an unwavering commitment to God's calling.

VICKI'S PERSONAL TESTIMONY

** "Will You Be What God Wants You to Be?"**

I am Vicki Jameson Peterson, and I want to invite you to be with me throughout this book. I have an interesting story to share, and I want to minister to you that you might be healed. You may be wondering, "Who are you?" That's a fair question. Thirty five years ago, I was called into ministry. At that time, I was just a homemaker, hungry for God, seeking the Lord with all my heart, praying, and helping others to begin their own ministries.

I thought that whenever I opened the Bible, the scripture that stood out to me was just a nice message for the moment. It didn't occur to me that it was the Spirit of the Lord dealing with me, preparing me for a ministry of singing and healing. I didn't realize then that He was calling me to be used in such a way.

As I share my story, I feel led to bring a scripture to you from the Book of Acts. It is found in **Acts 10:38 (KJV): "How God anointed Jesus of Nazareth with the Holy Ghost and with power: who went about doing good, and healing all that were oppressed of the devil; for God was with him."** The ministry of Jesus was closely tied to healing, and I believe He desires to heal you today, just as He did when He walked the earth.

My upbringing taught me to believe that God *could* heal, but it wasn't until I found myself in a hospital bed, gravely ill, that I began to truly grasp His willingness to heal. I wasn't sick because God made me sick, but through the sickness, my focus was sharpened on the Lord. I cried out to Him, feeling like such a failure, embarrassed even, thinking, "Oh God, I've failed You so badly. I'm supposed to be full of faith, yet here I am in a hospital."

Vicki Jamison Peterson: God's Anointed Vessel

In those difficult days, I learned that God is not limited by our circumstances. He always has a way if we just ask Him. He opens doors, makes provisions, and sends people with a word to heal and set us free. I experienced this firsthand when I suffered blood clots in my lungs and endured months of hospitalization. It was five o'clock one morning when I heard a voice—not audibly, but it was so real that it felt like it could have been.

The voice asked me some questions without any preface or buildup. There was no music, no scripture to set the tone—just these three simple yet profound questions: "Will you do what I want you to do? Will you be what I want you to be?"

God's healing is still available today, just as it was when Jesus walked the earth. If you are struggling, I encourage you to seek Him earnestly, believing in His power to heal and deliver. Remember, as it says in **Jeremiah 30:17 (KJV), "For I will restore health unto thee, and I will heal thee of thy wounds, saith the Lord."** Let His Word minister to you and bring the healing that only He can provide.

"The Cloud of His Glory: A Divine Encounter"

It was a life-changing moment when the Holy Spirit asked me, "Will you go where I want you to go?" I knew it was the voice of the Lord, and I responded with a heartfelt "Yes." As soon as I said yes, I had an unshakable knowing. When God calls you, He opens doors that no one else can. Soon after, I received an invitation to speak at the Full Gospel Businessmen's Regional Convention in Dallas, Texas, for the women's luncheon.

What an interesting day that was! I found myself standing before several hundred women, many of whom knew me personally. As I stood to speak, I didn't have a prepared message. All I knew was that I served a wonderful God who could do great things if we would just let Him. After all, He had already raised me up from a life-threatening condition. I began by thanking the women who had prayed for me, saying, "Thank you for your prayers. But don't blame God for what happened to me."

As I spoke those words, I happened to glance up and, with my spiritual eyes, saw a cloud. It may sound strange to some, but it was as real as the room I stood in. Intrigued, I repeated, "Don't blame God for what happened to me." The cloud descended lower, coming closer. I said it a third time, and then suddenly, I found myself enveloped in that cloud. A boldness came over me, and I declared to the women in the chandelier-adorned ballroom of the Statler Hilton, "If you want to know Jesus, if you want to be filled with the Spirit, if you want to be healed, please come to the front."

Without any exaggeration, women sprang from their seats and rushed to the front, standing two, three, and even four deep across the entire area. As I approached the first woman to lay hands on her, I hadn't even touched

Vicki Jamison Peterson: God's Anointed Vessel

her when the power of God came upon her, and she fell to the floor. I was astonished, yet the cloud of His glory was still there, surrounding me.

I stretched out my arm, and as I did, I was guided by an unseen force to gesture in the direction of the women waiting for prayer. It wasn't something I consciously planned to do; it just happened. The moment I made that gesture, the power of God swept through the room, and all the women fell under His mighty presence—thirty, forty, maybe even more—like a wave. The weight of God's glory was so strong that I, too, fell among them, unable to stand under the power of the Almighty.

This experience reminds me of the scripture in **Acts 2:17 (KJV): "And it shall come to pass in the last days, saith God, I will pour out of my Spirit upon all flesh."** Truly, the Lord is still pouring out His Spirit today, and His power is available to heal, to deliver, and to fill us with His presence. As it is written in **2 Corinthians 3:17 (KJV), "Now the Lord is that Spirit: and where the Spirit of the Lord is, there is liberty."** Let us open our hearts to the cloud of His glory, for He is still moving in our midst, longing to touch and transform our lives.

"A Homemaker in the Hands of God: The Outpouring of His Glory"

As the miraculous unfolded. Sharon Troley, who was at the piano that day, was playing as the Holy Spirit moved. They helped me to stay on my feet (for the glory of God was heavy on me) they guided me down the aisle where the women stood, and one after another, they fell under the power of God's glory. It was a sight to behold as the Lord healed ailments and set women free, right there in the midst of us. It was unlike anything I had ever witnessed or could have ever expected to be a part of.

I was just a homemaker without any formal education, and suddenly I found myself in the middle of a divine visitation. The Holy Spirit's presence was so real, so overwhelming, that it surpassed anything experienced through the senses—touch, feel, or smell. This was God in His splendor, manifesting His power in ways I could hardly comprehend. As I moved through the auditorium, women fell under the tables, over the tables, and some lay on the floor basking in the glory of God. At times, there were hundreds on the floor—100 to 200—completely overtaken by His presence.

Even the waiters and waitresses, distracted by the commotion, rushed in to see what was happening. When they did, they too fell under the power of God. It was beyond anything I had ever experienced, and even to this day, I have not seen that kind of power demonstrated in one meeting again. I suppose I would have never believed that God could use someone like me—just a homemaker—but He chooses whom He wills, and He empowers whom He calls.

Vicki Jamison Peterson: God's Anointed Vessel

This incredible experience reminds me of **1 Corinthians 1:27-29 (KJV): "But God hath chosen the foolish things of the world to confound the wise; and God hath chosen the weak things of the world to confound the things which are mighty; And base things of the world, and things which are despised, hath God chosen, yea, and things which are not, to bring to nought things that are: That no flesh should glory in his presence."** Truly, God's power is not limited by our status, background, or abilities. When He chooses to use someone, He does so in His own magnificent way.

Let us also remember what Jesus said in **John 14:12 (KJV): "Verily, verily, I say unto you, He that believeth on me, the works that I do shall he do also; and greater works than these shall he do; because I go unto my Father."** The Holy Spirit is still working mightily in the lives of believers, ready to use anyone who is willing to say "Yes" to His call.

"A Life of Faith: The Ministry and Legacy of Vicki Jamison Peterson"

Vibrant, gracious, determined, unconventional, joyful—these are just a few of the words that have been used to describe Vicki Jamison Peterson. Over the course of her 35-year ministry, Vicki powerfully demonstrated the gospel of Jesus Christ, bringing hope, healing, and transformation to countless lives. Her ministry took her across the globe, from England and Switzerland to

Australia, Germany, and beyond. As an evangelist and soul-winner, she was instrumental in leading over 20,000 people to Christ during crusades in New England, with many new churches being planted as a result.

In Chicago, Vicki founded a ministry called New Day House, an outreach that provided housing and support for unwed mothers and their children. She was also the author of several books on Christian living, including *El Shaddai* and *How You Can Have Joy*. As a gifted vocalist and psalmist, Vicki wrote numerous songs and recorded eight albums. Her pioneering work extended into Christian radio and television, where she produced two programs, *It's a New Day* and *Vicki Live*, while appearing as a regular guest on major Christian networks.

Her ministry was not easily categorized, as her influence transcended Christian denominations and movements. Vicki broke down racial, gender, and cultural barriers. In South Africa, she became the first person to hold interracial worship services after the end of apartheid, demonstrating her commitment to unity and reconciliation. As a trailblazer for women in ministry, Vicki paved the way for the women of today to take their rightful place in the body of Christ.

Through her ministry, the sick were healed, the oppressed were delivered, and men and women of all backgrounds encountered the life-changing power of the living God. Yet, true to her character, Vicki never sought praise for herself. She always pointed people to the Lord, insisting that all the glory belonged to Him alone.

Vicki Jamison Peterson: God's Anointed Vessel

As you reflect on Vicki's life and ministry, you will witness more than just the accomplishments of an individual. You will see God's power actively at work in the world, revealing His glory and transforming lives. **Vicki's message remains clear:** It is not head faith but heart faith that makes the difference. It is not mind over matter, but rather the Word of God ruling in your life.

As Vicki often emphasized, "If you'll get the Word of God on the inside of you and begin to think what the Word of God says instead of what your circumstances say, then the Word of God is going to come out in the crisis hour of your life." This echoes the promise found in **Mark 11:24 (KJV): "Therefore I say unto you, What things soever ye desire, when ye pray, believe that ye receive them, and ye shall have them."**

When the Word of God is in your heart, it brings joy even before the answer appears, for you know that the power of God is present to meet your need. Let this journey through Vicki's life and ministry inspire you to experience His presence in a deeper way and trust in His power to work mightily in your life as well.

"The Joy of Divine Protection: Testimonies of Healing and God's Miraculous Hand"

I want to introduce you to some very special friends with an incredible story to share. It was only a few months ago that they attended a meeting in this very auditorium, seated over to my right. That night, something extraordinary happened.

As I was calling out healings for different conditions, I said, "Someone has been healed of a hernia. You may not be ready to accept this or admit it, but you have been healed." I continued, "And right next to you, someone has been healed of asthma." At that moment, Jason turned to his grandmother and said, "Grandmother, that's us. Let's get up and go!" Being raised in a Lutheran church, where such things were unfamiliar, she hesitated. But when Jason insisted, "If you don't go with me, I'm going alone," she decided to join him.

They came down front, and as I prayed, God moved mightily. Jason was healed of asthma, and his grandmother was healed of the hernia. Afterwards, we went into a room where people were praying, some speaking in tongues, and others being "slain in the Spirit." It was a powerful scene. Suddenly, I heard a little voice beside me—it was Jason, his hands raised, speaking in an African dialect just as I had prayed earlier. It was a sign of God's miraculous touch upon his life.

A month later, I traveled to Tulsa, Oklahoma, with my parents. As we left the driveway, we declared, "In the name of Jesus, we appropriate the 91st Psalm." If you're unfamiliar with this passage, I encourage you to look it up. **Psalm 91 (KJV)** promises God's protection to all who trust in Him: **"He that dwelleth in the secret place of the most High shall abide under the shadow of the Almighty" (Psalm 91:1).** We claimed that promise for our journey.

Vicki Jamison Peterson: God's Anointed Vessel

Driving north on Highway 75 from Dallas toward Tulsa, we passed through a small town called Colgate. Somehow, I missed the highway marker. I noticed when the road became narrow, filled with holes, and weeds began to grow in the cracks. I realized I was lost and said to my mother, "I've missed Highway 75." Consulting the map, I found we were on Farm Road 331. I decided to take a shortcut to reconnect with Highway 75, but the road turned from hardtop to dirt, and I found myself driving on a narrow, bumpy path.

For about 30 minutes, I felt frustrated and hurried, thinking, "How could I have been so careless?" But when we finally pulled up onto Highway 75 again, we hadn't driven more than 10 minutes before we encountered cars and trucks stopped ahead. I saw a man standing on the road and asked, "What happened?" He replied, "A bridge collapsed in three places about 30 minutes ago. A truck was buried in the sand, and another had crashed at the bottom."

Stunned, I realized that if I hadn't been lost on that detour, we would have arrived at the collapsed bridge exactly 30 minutes earlier. I looked at the man and said, "Do you believe in miracles?" It was then that the joy of the Lord began to well up inside me. As **Proverbs 3:6 (KJV)** reminds us, **"In all thy ways acknowledge him, and he shall direct thy paths."** We started a spontaneous prayer meeting right in the car, praising God for His protection.

God's Word is indeed powerful, and His promises are true. As **Romans 8:28 (KJV)** assures us, **"And we know**

that all things work together for good to them that love God, to them who are the called according to his purpose." This experience taught me that even in our mistakes, God's hand is at work, guiding us and keeping us safe.

God has done marvelous things, and His joy is evident in the lives of those He touches. I can see that same joy in you today, and it radiates from your face. Let us always rejoice in His keeping power and share the testimonies of His wonderful works!

DR MICAEL H YEAGER
AUTHORS SUPERNATURAL EXPERIENCE

** Saved by Divine Unction: A Miracle at the Mississippi River**

On August 1, 2007, my family and I set out on what we thought would be an ordinary day of vacation, driving westward toward Yellowstone National Park. In the truck with me were my wife, my three sons, and my daughter. We were pulling a 35-foot fifth-wheel trailer with our Toyota crew cab, taking in the beauty of the open road. Little did we know that we were on a collision course with disaster—or at least, we would have been, had it not been for a divine intervention.

We were traveling along Highway I-35 West, heading through downtown Minneapolis, Minnesota. It was the middle of the day, and everything seemed normal. Our

Vicki Jamison Peterson: God's Anointed Vessel

GPS was directing us, guiding us along the quickest route to our destination. But suddenly, something stirred inside me—a powerful sense of urgency. I've had vivid experiences like this before, moments where I perceive that God is about to do something significant or that something is about to happen. And this time, I knew it was serious.

As I was driving, an overwhelming feeling rose up inside me, what I would call a divine unction of the Holy Ghost. It wasn't just a simple gut feeling. It was deeper, more powerful a pressing urgency that surged up from within, telling me that we needed to get off the highway. I had learned over the years to trust this leading of the Spirit, and I knew that this was one of those times when immediate obedience was necessary.

I turned to my family and said, "Something's wrong. We need to get off this highway now." They looked at me with concern, but they knew from our past experiences that when I said something like this, it wasn't to be taken lightly. They said: Dad obey God! Our family was used to following the guidance of the Holy Spirit, and this time was no different.

Without hesitation, I took the nearest exit. Our GPS protested, trying to reroute us back onto I-35 West, but I ignored it. Instead, we began heading north, following a less direct route. After driving for a while, we eventually connected to another highway and continued our journey westward. By then, the sense of urgency had faded, and the road felt peaceful again.

Later that day, we pulled into a store to take a break. As

we walked inside, we noticed a small crowd gathered around a television. The mood in the room was tense, and people were glued to the screen. Curious, we walked over to see what was going on. The images on the TV were shocking devastation over the Mississippi River. A bridge had collapsed earlier that day, with vehicles plunging into the water below. The news anchors were reporting on the tragedy, showing the wreckage of cars, trucks, and buses scattered in the river.

I stared at the screen, my heart pounding as the realization hit me like a wave. The bridge that had collapsed was part of Highway I-35 West—the very road we had been on before the Holy Ghost urged me to exit. If we hadn't gotten off the highway when we did, we would have been on that bridge, right in the middle of the collapse. Thirteen people lost their lives that day, and 145 were seriously injured. The images of twisted metal and submerged vehicles were haunting.

Only God knows what might have happened to us had I not obeyed that unction. Would we have survived? Would we have been among those seriously injured or worse? I'll never know for sure, but one thing I do know: the Lord delivered us that day. It wasn't chance or luck; it was divine intervention. The Holy Spirit had quickened my heart, and in that moment, obedience saved our lives.

As I reflected on what had happened, the words of 2 **Timothy 4:17** came to my mind: **"Notwithstanding the Lord stood with me, and strengthened me; that by me the preaching might be fully known, and that all the Gentiles might hear: and I was delivered out of the mouth of the lion."** Just as the Lord stood with Paul,

Vicki Jamison Peterson: God's Anointed Vessel

delivering him from peril, I knew that God had stood with me and my family that day. He had strengthened me with a word of warning and guided us to safety.

This experience was a powerful reminder of the many ways God speaks and leads us. Sometimes it's through His Word, other times through the counsel of others, and often through the inner prompting of the Holy Spirit. That day, it was the still, small voice of the Spirit that saved us from potential tragedy.

It's a reminder that we must be sensitive to His leading, even when it doesn't make sense in the moment. The road we were on seemed perfectly safe, and by all appearances, there was no danger ahead. But God, in His infinite wisdom, knew what was coming and guided us away from harm.

I thank the Lord for His protection that day, for sparing my family and me from a terrible fate. We serve a God who sees what we cannot, and who in His love, guides us through every danger. Let us never take for granted His presence with us, for as He promised, "Lo, I am with you alway, even unto the end" (Matthew 28:20). And truly, He is.

CHAPTER TWO
"Healing and Hope: Reaching Forward in Christ"

In March of 1975, a remarkable healing took place. One night, while watching a program on PTL, a woman found herself experiencing the miraculous. Vicki was calling out healings, and as this woman got up from her chair to adjust the TV volume, she heard Vicki say, "Lady, you're bending in front of your TV set—you're healed of lupus. I don't really know what that is, but claim your healing, you're healed." At that moment, the woman claimed her healing by faith.

She had been diagnosed with lupus, an incurable disease according to medical science. But we know that with God, nothing is impossible. Over a year later, she remained completely free from any symptoms of the disease. With joy in her heart, she could now testify, "I certainly am joyful. I have something to be joyful about!" We give God all the glory for her healing.

Many people are held captive by the hurts and

Vicki Jamison Peterson: God's Anointed Vessel

disappointments of the past. Vicki learned the importance of moving beyond yesterday's pain and reaching ahead toward the destiny God has for each of us. This was not just a message she preached; it was a truth she lived out. In the following clip, she shares how we must allow God to heal the wounds of our past so that we can find peace in the present and embrace the glorious future that awaits.

The Apostle Paul reminds us in **Philippians 3:13-14 (KJV): "Brethren, I count not myself to have apprehended: but this one thing I do, forgetting those things which are behind, and reaching forth unto those things which are before, I press toward the mark for the prize of the high calling of God in Christ Jesus."**

Forgetting the past is not about ignoring what happened, but rather, it is about surrendering it to God and allowing Him to bring healing. When we do, we can press forward toward the goal that He has set before us. The burdens and heartaches lose their grip as we trust in Christ's power to transform our lives.

Vicki's testimony and ministry continue to remind us that God is able to heal, deliver, and set us free. As we press on, we can trust that His healing touch is still available, and His power is as real today as it was then. Let us embrace the joy of our salvation and the hope of our future, knowing that the Lord is faithful to complete the good work He has begun in us **(Philippians 1:6, KJV): "Being confident of this very thing, that he which hath begun a good work in you will perform it until** the day of Jesus Christ."

God calls each of us to move beyond yesterday's troubles, to find peace in the present, and to reach forward to the future He has prepared. Today, let go of the past and step into the healing and freedom that Christ offers. The best is yet to come!

** "Anointed for Wholeness: Vicki Jamison Peterson's Message of Faith in Christ"**

The energy in the auditorium was alive with expectation as Vicki Jamison Peterson took the stage, her voice steady yet filled with conviction. She believed that the Word of God, once sown in good soil, would sprout and build faith in every heart present. "Tonight, you're not going to leave this place the same," she declared, her eyes shining. "God's Word will stir something deep in you—it's going to change you." Then she paused, lifting a prayer that left the room in silent awe. "Father, in the name of Jesus, let Your Word come alive in our hearts. Thank You that Your Word is forever settled in heaven, and that each one here will know You are an unlimited God, ready to bring wholeness into our lives."

The crowd whispered their agreement, a soft murmur of "Amen" sweeping through as she continued. "Now, let's declare this truth together," she encouraged, "Say it after me—'God is a good God. God is a healing God. God loves me.'" The room was filled with the sound of hundreds of voices repeating those words, louder and more confident with each phrase. She urged them to turn

Vicki Jamison Peterson: God's Anointed Vessel

to one another, "Tell your neighbor, 'God loves you!'" The sound of faith being spoken out loud created an undeniable atmosphere of hope.

Vicki then opened her Bible to the book of John, chapter 1, verses 32 and 33, reading with purpose. "John testified, **'I saw the Spirit descending like a dove out of heaven, and it remained on Him.'** This was the moment that changed everything for Jesus. He was the Son of God, the Son of Man, but until that day, there were no miracles, no signs, no wonders." She paused to let her words sink in. "But when the Holy Spirit came upon Him at the river Jordan, the power of God began to flow, and miracles followed. This is the anointing of the Holy Spirit, and it's vital to our own wholeness."

Explaining the significance of Jesus' baptism and the anointing He received, Vicki highlighted the essence of the Spirit's power in the life of every believer. She shared how Jesus' ministry began with the Spirit's anointing—a clear signal that, as she put it, "We can do nothing on our own, but through Him, all things are possible." She referenced **Isaiah 10:27, "And it shall come to pass in that day, that his burden shall be taken away from off thy shoulder, and his yoke from off thy neck, and the yoke shall be destroyed because of the anointing."** For Vicki, this was more than a scripture; it was a promise that the Holy Spirit's presence in a believer's life breaks every chain, every yoke of bondage.

As Vicki continued, she led the audience deeper into understanding that Jesus' power wasn't just for Him but was meant for everyone who believes. "The same Spirit that empowered Jesus now dwells within us," she assured them, referencing **Romans 8:11, "But if the Spirit of him that raised up Jesus from the dead dwell in you, he that raised up Christ from the dead shall also quicken your mortal bodies."** This wasn't simply a matter of theology to her; it was an invitation to experience the wholeness God desires for His people. Each testimony she shared brought to life the reality of God's healing power, recounting miracles she had witnessed sicknesses healed, lives restored, and burdens lifted.

Near the end, she led a final prayer, asking God to release His Spirit over the room, "Lord, let Your anointing fall like it did on Jesus. Let Your healing power work in our lives, our bodies, and our families. In Jesus' name, we proclaim it done." The room echoed with voices declaring, "Done!" Vicki's faith, passion, and anointing left no doubt—each person there was invited to embrace a deeper life in Jesus, empowered by the Spirit and anointed for God's purpose. Through her ministry, they didn't just learn about God's power; they encountered it.

Vicki's legacy lives on in the stories of those transformed through her faith-filled teaching and the love of Jesus she shared. Her message was simple yet profound: the Holy Spirit's anointing is available to every believer, bringing healing, wholeness, and the power to live victoriously. And in her own words, **"God is a good God, a healing God, and He loves you."**

****"The Anointing of the Holy Spirit:**

Vicki Jamison Peterson: God's Anointed Vessel

Transforming Lives Through Faith"**

In this discourse, we delve into the transformative power of God's Word, akin to the parable of the sower where Jesus spoke of the seed falling on good soil, representing hearts ready to receive and grow in faith. As Jesus taught in **Matthew 13:23**, "But he that received seed into the good ground is he that heareth the word, and understandeth it; which also beareth fruit, and bringeth forth, some an hundredfold, some sixty, some thirty." This scripture aligns with our belief that the Word, when received, will not leave us unchanged.

The prayer for divine empowerment is echoed in **Philippians 4:13**, "I can do all things through Christ which strengtheneth me," reminding us that through Jesus, we are endowed with strength, power, and vigor to face life's challenges.

We acknowledge God's unchangeable nature as stated in **Psalm 119:89**, "For ever, O LORD, thy word is settled in heaven," which assures us that God's promises and His Word are steadfast, providing a foundation for our faith and healing.

When we affirm together, "God is a good God," we are reminded of **Psalm 34:8**, "O taste and see that the LORD is good: blessed is the man that trusteth in him," encouraging a personal experience of God's goodness.

The anointing of the Holy Spirit, pivotal in our spiritual

journey, is beautifully illustrated in **John 1:32-33** where John the Baptist testifies, **"And John bare record, saying, I saw the Spirit descending from heaven like a dove, and it abode upon him. And I knew him not: but he that sent me to baptize with water, the same said unto me, Upon whom thou shalt see the Spirit descending, and remaining on him, the same is he which baptizeth with the Holy Ghost."** This scripture underlines the moment when Jesus, upon receiving the Holy Spirit, began His miraculous ministry, showing us the importance of the Holy Spirit in our lives for ministry and personal transformation.

Acts 10:38 further elaborates, **"How God anointed Jesus of Nazareth with the Holy Ghost and with power: who went about doing good, and healing all that were oppressed of the devil; for God was with him."** This verse connects Jesus' ministry with the anointing of the Holy Spirit, emphasizing that our own empowerment and healing are linked to this divine anointing.

Let us remember that Jesus, the Son of God, started His public ministry not by His own will but through the anointing of the Holy Spirit. This anointing should encourage us to seek not only personal healing but also to engage in the ministry of reconciliation and healing for others, as Jesus did, knowing that **"the Spirit of the Lord is upon me, because he hath anointed me to preach the gospel to the poor; he hath sent me to heal the brokenhearted, to preach deliverance to the captives, and recovering of sight to the blind, to set at liberty them that are bruised"** (**Luke 4:18**).

Vicki Jamison Peterson: God's Anointed Vessel

As we explore the life of Jesus post-baptism, we see Him led by the Holy Spirit into the wilderness, where He faced temptation, yet triumphed through the power of the Spirit. This mirrors our own spiritual journeys, where we too must overcome temptations, bolstered by the Holy Spirit within us, as exemplified by **1 John 4:4: "Ye are of God, little children, and have overcome them: because greater is he that is in you, than he that is in the world."**

Upon returning from the wilderness, Jesus began His ministry, driven by the anointing of the Holy Spirit. In **Luke 4:18-19**, He reads from Isaiah, declaring, **"The Spirit of the Lord is upon me, because he hath anointed me to preach the gospel to the poor; he hath sent me to heal the brokenhearted, to preach deliverance to the captives, and recovering of sight to the blind, to set at liberty them that are bruised, To preach the acceptable year of the Lord."** Here, Jesus not only identifies Himself as the Messiah but also outlines His mission, which is now ours through the same Spirit.

The term "anointed" as Jesus used it, signifies being equipped and empowered for a divine purpose. This anointing is not merely symbolic but actively "furnishes what is needed," as per the explanation of the Greek word used. This understanding aligns with **Philippians 2:13: "For it is God which worketh in you both to will and to do of his good pleasure,"** highlighting that the anointing empowers us to fulfill God's will.

Romans 8:11 further solidifies this concept, **"But if the Spirit of him that raised up Jesus from the dead dwell in you, he that raised up Christ from the dead shall also quicken your mortal bodies by his Spirit that dwelleth in you."** This scripture reassures us that the same power that resurrected Jesus is actively working within us, not only for spiritual renewal but also for physical and emotional healing.

The anointing, therefore, is not a passive event but an active engagement with the Holy Spirit, equipping us for service, healing, and deliverance. As Jesus was anointed to fulfill His ministry, so are we anointed to carry out His mission in the world today.

Let us embrace this anointing, acknowledging that through the Spirit who dwells in us, we are empowered to live out the mission of Christ, bringing good news, healing, and liberation to all who are oppressed or in need. May we walk in this truth, confident that the Spirit of God is actively working within us, furnishing all that is needed for our journey and ministry.

****"The Gifts of the Spirit: Empowering the Faithful"****

We see that it's the Spirit who raised Christ from the dead, and it is this Spirit who works through the anointing **(Romans 8:11, "But if the Spirit of him that raised up Jesus from the dead dwell in you, he that**

Vicki Jamison Peterson: God's Anointed Vessel

raised up Christ from the dead shall also quicken your mortal bodies by his Spirit that dwelleth in you"). This anointing is of the Spirit, and as we examine special anointings, we are directed to 1 Corinthians 12.

Paul begins in **1 Corinthians 12:1, "Now concerning spiritual gifts, brethren, I would not have you ignorant."** The Amplified Bible adds clarity, referring to these gifts as **"special endowments of supernatural energy."** Paul underscores that these gifts—endowments of supernatural power—should not be misunderstood or ignored. In verse 4, we read that **"there are diversities of gifts, but the same Spirit" (1 Corinthians 12:4, KJV),** which highlights the variety within the unity of the Spirit's work. Among these are the "power gifts": the gift of faith, the gift of healing, and the working of miracles.

When ministering in a service, we may observe the gift of faith in action, often moving the hearts of unbelievers to receive their healings due to the collective faith present. Jesus said in **Matthew 18:20, "For where two or three are gathered together in my name, there am I in the midst of them,"** and it is in such gatherings that a collective faith blesses everyone in attendance, even unbelievers. The Spirit works through each believer as He wills, sometimes gifting us with faith beyond our natural capacity.

In **Romans 12:3**, Paul reminds us that **"God hath dealt to every man the measure of faith,"** but there are moments when an extraordinary gift of faith "drops" upon us. Have you ever experienced a surge in faith, where you felt you could believe beyond belief? Consider a time when a woman came forward with severe pain in her gums and chin. The Spirit prompted the gift of faith, and over the course of 45 minutes, her pain subsided, and numb areas regained sensation. The healing took time, yet faith persisted. As **James 5:15** declares, **"And the prayer of faith shall save the sick, and the Lord shall raise him up."**

Why does this gift manifest sometimes and not others? Scripture teaches us that it is **"the same Spirit, which worketh all in all" (1 Corinthians 12:6, KJV),** and it is **"as the Spirit wills" (1 Corinthians 12:11, KJV).** We might not understand it fully, but as we yield to the Spirit, we open ourselves to further revelation. Those studying for ministry are encouraged to lay hands on the sick in faith, as **"they shall lay hands on the sick, and they shall recover" (Mark 16:18, KJV).** This is not limited to those in formal ministry but extends to all believers, for it is the Spirit who empowers.

The gifts of the Spirit work as God wills, whether in the singular "gift of healing" or "gifts of healings." Jesus Himself showed that healing was an essential part of His ministry, **"And he laid his hands on every one of them and healed them" (Luke 4:40, KJV).** The Spirit's power flows through these gifts, whether we emphasize the plural or singular, as it is our obedience and heart that matter most.

At times as I sang, the word of knowledge and the word of wisdom were also present. The word of knowledge provides insight into past or present events, while the

Vicki Jamison Peterson: God's Anointed Vessel

word of wisdom speaks to future direction. Some receive one gift, others may operate in multiple gifts, and all are empowered by the Spirit's will. Miracles, such as Jesus turning water into wine **(John 2:1-11),** reflect divine intervention beyond healing, demonstrating God's supernatural power in both the natural and physical realms.

Beloved, let us seek earnestly these gifts, understanding their purpose and power. **"But covet earnestly the best gifts" (1 Corinthians 12:31, KJV),** for it is the Spirit who endows us, equipping us for service and bearing witness to the supernatural God we serve.

** "Miracles of Faith: Witnessing the Creative Power of God Through Spiritual Gifts"**

In one service, a woman came forward with a unique request: she wanted her finger, cut off at the first joint, to be healed. Naturally, we cannot restore what isn't there by human ability. However, with the faith present, we obeyed the Word and commanded her finger to grow in Jesus' name. To my astonishment, the finger began to grow out! I was as surprised as anyone else, for it was entirely the work of God, demonstrating the mighty power of His Spirit. As Jesus said in **Mark 9:23, "If thou canst believe, all things are possible to him that believeth."**

This miracle was witnessed not only by believers but also by a skeptical banker, showcasing that signs and wonders serve as evidence to the unbelieving world. Miracles like these remind us of God's supernatural ability to work beyond human expectation, as expressed in **Acts 4:30, "By stretching forth thine hand to heal; and that signs and wonders may be done by the name of thy holy child Jesus."** Similarly, the Lord has performed other creative miracles, such as lengthening legs and recreating parts of the body, showing us that **"Jesus Christ the same yesterday, and to day, and for ever" (Hebrews 13:8).**

In **1 Corinthians 12:28,** we read about the divine appointments within the church: **"And God hath set some in the church, first apostles, secondarily prophets, thirdly teachers, after that miracles, then gifts of healings, helps, governments, diversities of tongues."** Here, Paul emphasizes that God specifically ordains some individuals with distinct gifts, including wonder-working power and healing. The Spirit asks in **1 Corinthians 12:30, "Have all the gifts of healing? do all speak with tongues? do all interpret?"** The rhetorical question makes it clear that not everyone operates in these gifts, which are given as the Spirit wills, to glorify God rather than to bring attention to any individual.

It's crucial to remember that these gifts are for the edification and glorification of God alone. When the Spirit operates through us, we must direct all honor to Him, as seen in **1 Peter 4:11: "If any man speak, let him speak as the oracles of God; if any man minister, let him do it as of the ability which God giveth: that God in all things may be glorified through Jesus Christ."** The gifts should never bring glory to the person,

Vicki Jamison Peterson: God's Anointed Vessel

but rather to God, who is the true source of all miracles. The Spirit distributes these gifts to fulfill God's purpose, just as Jesus Himself declared in **John 14:13, "And whatsoever ye shall ask in my name, that will I do, that the Father may be glorified in the Son."**

Through these miracles, God demonstrates His presence among us, as a continual testament to His love and power. Let us yield to the Spirit, trust in His will, and always give glory to the one true God who works all things for His glory.

"The Power and Purpose of the Holy Spirit in Jesus and the Early Church"

Something remarkable happened in the early church, revealing the power of the Spirit's anointing. Let's look at **Acts 4:27-31**, where the church prayed together with one heart, invoking the name of Jesus. Verse 27 declares, **"For of a truth against thy holy child Jesus, whom thou hast anointed, both Herod, and Pontius Pilate, with the Gentiles, and the people of Israel, were gathered together."** Notice how they recognized Jesus as the "holy child" anointed by God, and they understood the authority that came from this anointing.

The power of the name of Jesus is essential; **Philippians 2:9-10** states, **"Wherefore God also hath highly exalted him, and given him a name which is above every name: That at the name of Jesus every knee should bow."** Through His anointing, Jesus was consecrated for a unique purpose, embodying the fullness of God's authority. In **Acts 4:30-31**, we read how the disciples prayed, **"By stretching forth thine hand to heal; and that signs and wonders may be done by the name of thy holy child Jesus."** As they prayed in unity, the place where they gathered was shaken, and they were filled with the Holy Ghost, boldly proclaiming the Word of God.

This passage shows the importance of collective prayer and unity in seeking God's power. As **Matthew 18:19-20** affirms, **"Again I say unto you, That if two of you shall agree on earth as touching any thing that they shall ask, it shall be done for them of my Father which is in heaven. For where two or three are gathered together in my name, there am I in the midst of them."** In these moments, the Spirit empowers believers to fulfill the will of God with boldness and courage, just as Jesus was anointed to do.

In the ministry of Jesus, we see the importance of this anointing clearly. **Luke 5:17** tells us of a powerful moment, saying, **"And it came to pass on a certain day, as he was teaching, that there were Pharisees and doctors of the law sitting by, which were come out of every town of Galilee, and Judaea, and Jerusalem: and the power of the Lord was present to heal them."** The Spirit's anointing was with Jesus, enabling Him to teach, heal, and manifest God's power wherever He went. This same Spirit anoints us, empowering us to carry out God's work on earth.

Reflecting on the ministry of Jesus, it becomes clear that

Vicki Jamison Peterson: God's Anointed Vessel

the greatest pursuit we can have is to know Him. As Jesus said in **John 17:3, "And this is life eternal, that they might know thee the only true God, and Jesus Christ, whom thou hast sent."** The more we study His life, the closer we draw to Him, and as we grow in our knowledge of Him, we reflect His character more fully. **Romans 8:29** reveals our ultimate destiny: **"For whom he did foreknow, he also did predestinate to be conformed to the image of his Son."** Our calling isn't to pursue greatness but to pursue Christlikeness, becoming vessels through which His Spirit flows.

This potential resides in each believer, as we are reminded in **2 Peter 1:3, "According as his divine power hath given unto us all things that pertain unto life and godliness, through the knowledge of him that hath called us to glory and virtue."** It's a process, requiring choices and perseverance, but as **Philippians 1:6** assures, we can be **"confident of this very thing, that he which hath begun a good work in you will perform it until the day of Jesus Christ."**

In our journey, let us be encouraged, pressing forward with the confidence that the same Spirit who anointed Jesus lives in us, equipping and empowering us to fulfill His purposes, as we yield ourselves to Him.

DR MICAEL H YEAGER
AUTHORS SUPERNATURAL EXPERIENCE

Healed When I Slammed My Broken Foot Down the 5th Time.

One day I had to climb our 250-foot AM radio tower to change the light bulb on the main beacon. (If you ever visit our church I will be glad to have you visit our tower) However, to climb the tower, I had to first find the keys, which I never did. Since I could not find the keys to get the fence open, I did the next best thing—I simply climbed over the fence.

This idea turned out not to be such a wonderful idea after all! With all my climbing gear hanging from my waist, I climbed the fence to the very top. At this point, my rope gear became entangled in the fencing. As I tried to get free, I lost my balance and fell backwards off the fence. Trying to break my fall, I got my right foot down underneath me. I hit the ground with my foot being turned on its side and I felt something snap in the ankle. I knew instantly I had a broken foot, my ankle.

Most normal people would have climbed back over the fence, go set up a doctor's appointment, have their foot x rayed, and then placed into a cast. But I am not a normal-thinking person, at least according to the standards of the modern-day church. When I broke my foot, I followed my routine of confessing my stupidity to God and asking Him to forgive me for my stupidity.

Moreover, then I spoke to my foot and commanded it to be healed in the name of Jesus Christ of Nazareth. When I had finished speaking to my foot, commanding it to be healed, and then praising and thanking God for the

Vicki Jamison Peterson: God's Anointed Vessel

healing, there seem to be no change whatsoever in its condition.

The Scripture that came to my heart was where Jesus declared, "The kingdom of heaven suffereth violence, and the violent take it by force!" Based completely upon this scripture, I decided to climb the tower by FAITH, with a broken foot mind you. Please do not misunderstand, my foot hurt so bad I could hardly stand it. And yet, I had declared that I BELIEVED I was healed.

There were three men watching me as I took the Word of God by FAITH. I told them what I was about to do, and they looked at me as if I had lost my mind. I began to climb the 250-foot tower, one painful step at a time.

My foot hurt so bad that I was hyperventilating within just twenty to thirty feet up the tower. It literally felt like I was going to pass out from shock at any moment. Whenever I got to the point of fainting, I would connect my climbing ropes to the tower, stop and take a breather, crying out to Jesus to help me. It seemed to take me forever to get to the top.

Even so, I finally did reach the very top of the tower and replaced the light bulb that had gone out. Usually, I can come down that tower within 10 minutes, because I would press my feet against the tower rods, and then slide down, just using my hands and arms to lower myself at a very fast pace.

However, in this situation, my foot could not handle the pressure of being pushed up against the steel.

Consequently, I had to work my way down very slowly. After I was down, I slowly climbed over the fence one more time. I hobbled my way over to my vehicle and drove up to the church office. The men who had been watching this unfold, were right behind me.

I hobbled my way into the front office, which is directly across the street from the radio tower. I informed the personnel that I had broken my foot, showing them my black and blue, extremely swollen foot. It did not help that I had climbed with it! I told them that I was going home to rest. At the same time, however, I told them that I BELIEVED I was healed.

Going to my house, which is directly across from the main office of the church parking lot, I made my way slowly up the stairs to our bedroom. I found my wife in the bedroom putting away our clothes. Slowly and painfully, I pulled the shoe and sock off the broken foot.

What a mess! It was fat, swollen, black and blue all over. I put a pillow down at the end of the bed, and carefully pulled myself up onto the bed. Lying on my back, I tenderly placed my broken, black, and blue, swollen foot onto the pillow. No matter how I positioned it, the pain did not cease. I just laid there squirming, moaning, and sighing.

As I was lying there trying to overcome the shock that kept hitting my body, I heard the audible voice of God. He said to me: "What are you doing in bed? God really got my attention when I heard him with my natural ears. My wife would testify that she heard nothing. Immediately in my heart I said: Lord I'm just resting.

Vicki Jamison Peterson: God's Anointed Vessel

Then He spoke to my heart with the still small voice very clearly, do you always rest at this time of day? No, Lord, I replied. (It was about 3 o'clock in the afternoon)

He spoke to my heart again and said: I thought you said you were healed by MY Stripes?

At that very moment I knew it was Jesus Himself talking to me and the gift of FAITH exploded inside my heart. I said, "Lord, I am healed! Immediately, I pushed myself up off the bed, grabbed my sock and shoe, and struggled to put them back on. What a tremendous struggle it was! My foot was so swollen that it did not want to go into the shoe. My wife was watching me as I fought to complete this task.

You might wonder what my wife was doing this whole time as I was fighting this battle of FAITH. She was doing what she always does, just watching me and shaking her head. I finally got the shoe on my swollen, black, and blue foot. I put my foot down on the floor and began to put my body weight upon it. When I did, I almost passed out. At that moment, a holy anger exploded on the inside of me. I declared out loud, "I am healed in the name of Jesus Christ of Nazareth!" With that declaration, I took my right (broken) foot and slammed it down to the floor as hard as I possibly could.

When I did that, I felt the bones of my foot break even more. Like the Fourth of July, an explosion of blue, purple, red, white, black exploded in my brain and I passed out. I came to lying on my bed. Afterward, my wife informed me that every time I passed out, it was for about ten to twenty seconds.

The moment I came to, I jumped right back up out of bed. The gift of FAITH was working in me mightily. I got back up and followed the same process again, "In the name of Jesus Christ of Nazareth I am healed," and slammed my foot down once more as hard as I could! For a second time, I could feel the damage in my foot increasing. My mind was once again wrapped in an explosion of colors and pain as I blacked out.

When I regained consciousness, I immediately got up once again, repeating the same process. After the third time this happening I came to with my wife leaning over the top of me. I remember my wife saying as she looked at me, "You're making me sick. I can't watch you do this." She promptly walked out of our bedroom and went downstairs.

The fourth time I got up declaring, "In the name of Jesus Christ of Nazareth I am healed, "and slammed my foot even harder! Once more, multiple colors of intense pain hit my brain. I passed out again! I got up the fifth time, angrier than ever. This was not demonic or proud anger.

This was a divine gift of violent I-will-not-take-no-for-an-answer type of FAITH. I slammed my foot down the fifth time, "In the name of Jesus Christ of Nazareth I am healed!" The minute my foot slammed into the floor, for the fifth time, the power of God hit my foot. I literally stood there under the quickening power of God, and watched my foot shrink and become normal.

All the pain was completely and totally gone. I pulled back my sock and watched the black and blue in my foot disappear to normal flesh color. I was healed! Praise

Vicki Jamison Peterson: God's Anointed Vessel

God, I was made whole! I went back to the office, giving glory to the Lord and showing the staff my healed foot.

CHAPTER THREE

"The Presence of Healing: Unveiling the Power of Faith and the Anointing of Jesus"

The power of God was with Jesus, present to heal everyone gathered in His presence. As **Luke 5:17** states, **"And the power of the Lord was present to heal them."** But among the crowd, only one man—a paralyzed man brought by his friends—received healing. The story continues in verses **18-19**, describing how, when they could not enter because of the crowd, the friends lowered the man through the roof, right into the midst before Jesus. Observing their unwavering faith, Jesus declared, **"Man, thy sins are forgiven thee" (Luke 5:20).**

Then, in **Luke 5:24**, Jesus affirmed His divine authority, saying, **"But that ye may know that the Son of man hath power upon earth to forgive sins, (he said unto the sick of the palsy,) I say unto thee, Arise, and take up thy couch, and go into thine house."** Immediately, the man stood up, took his mat, and went home, **"glorifying God" (Luke 5:25).** Although the power to

Vicki Jamison Peterson: God's Anointed Vessel

heal was present for all, only one received this miraculous touch, showing that faith must be combined with God's power for His works to manifest.

This scene illustrates that Jesus was anointed to heal, as foretold in **Isaiah 61:1, "The Spirit of the Lord GOD is upon me; because the LORD hath anointed me to preach good tidings unto the meek."** Through His anointing, Jesus demonstrated the power of God, revealing a truth we are called to embrace in our own lives.

In my own journey, I've come to understand a valuable truth—a "secret" learned through experience. As Paul wrote in **Philippians 4:11-12, "I have learned, in whatsoever state I am, therewith to be content. I know both how to be abased, and I know how to abound."** Recently, I encountered an unexpected illness that rapidly impacted my health. It was a surprise, and I struggled to understand it, but God, in His grace, began teaching me profound lessons about healing. He has brought me through many steps of healing, and I will share more later in this book about this journey. These steps have deepened my understanding of healing, faith, and the importance of trusting God through the process.

One aspect of this healing journey included a remarkable experience where God's wisdom worked through a Spirit-led doctor. **Proverbs 3:5-6 reminds us to "Trust in the LORD with all thine heart; and lean not unto thine own understanding. In all thy ways acknowledge him, and he shall direct thy paths."** It was through my husband, a specialist in brain chemistry, that God orchestrated my healing. God had long foreseen this need, preparing a way to restore my health. **Romans 8:28** assures us, **"And we know that all things work together for good to them that love God, to them who are the called according to his purpose."**

Through faith, prayer, and God's divine orchestration, I have learned much about healing. His foreknowledge prepared the way, just as He has done for each of us.

"Faith in Action: Walking in Healing Through God's Anointing and Divine Guidance"

There are many components to healing, including the word of knowledge and, sometimes, medication. I believe in taking medicine if it's recommended. Medicine itself isn't the miracle worker—my husband, like any doctor, would say that medicine supports healing but doesn't bring complete restoration. I did everything within my power, yet instead of improving, my health worsened. We prayed, believed, and thanked God, hoping the medicine would eventually help. In December, the doctor said it might take six months to see improvement, so we prepared for a long journey.

Interestingly, while I needed exercise to aid my recovery, another condition, revealed through the Holy Spirit to a doctor at the City of Faith, prevented me from exercising without causing harm. This delicate balance could have led to severe consequences if undetected. Had I not been living with my husband, who specializes in brain

Vicki Jamison Peterson: God's Anointed Vessel

chemistry, the condition might have gone unnoticed, resulting in my confinement to a nursing home or mental institution due to the effects of an untreated chemical imbalance. Isn't God clever and loving? God always works with us where we are at in our faith walk. He orchestrated every detail to ensure my healing journey was not missed.

In January, despite my health, I had a commitment to speak in California. Rex Berg, who has supported me for many years, my husband, and my staff all worked together to make this trip possible. My condition required considerable planning, but everyone stepped in to help with the challenges. When Rex arrived, he saw firsthand my struggle—I could barely walk, often leaning against walls for support. While I was mentally alert, communicating was difficult, making me realize the importance of showing grace to those with physical or mental challenges. **James 2:13** says, **"For he shall have judgment without mercy, that hath shewed no mercy; and mercy rejoiceth against judgment."** This experience taught me the value of patience and kindness, as people who appear limited are often more aware than they can express.

I was blessed by the love and support around me and never believed my illness would be permanent. I rose each morning, did my hair and makeup, and faced each day with determination. **James 2:17** reminds us, **"Even so faith, if it hath not works, is dead, being alone."** Living as though I were well, even if I had to hold onto walls, became part of my commitment to faith. In social situations, I often struggled to keep up with conversations; my friends eventually talked among themselves, understanding I couldn't contribute. While I knew what was happening around me, I felt imprisoned within myself, unable to express my thoughts.

When Rex saw me, I could barely walk, but I was committed to fulfill my speaking engagement. Faith requires action, and while it's easy to say, "Just believe," years of building my faith through God's Word had prepared me for this moment. Faith is alive, powerful, and energizing, and I knew I had to act on it. Within a week of Rex's arrival, I started walking more steadily. Though my muscles were weak from inactivity, I pressed on, confident that God was guiding me through each step.

By God's grace, I traveled to California, changing planes twice to reach my destination. Through the power of faith, prayer, and God's anointing, I witnessed His strength in my weakness. **2 Corinthians 12:9** assures us, **"And he said unto me, My grace is sufficient for thee: for my strength is made perfect in weakness."** Indeed, His strength carried me through when mine was not enough, showing that faith, medicine, and the anointing work together under God's divine hand.

"Faith in Action: Persevering Through Weakness with God's Anointing"

Be kind to the handicapped, for their situation may not be permanent if we trust in God's anointing. As believers, we are called to extend compassion, for they are human

Vicki Jamison Peterson: God's Anointed Vessel

beings with feelings and understanding. **Romans 15:1** reminds us, **"We then that are strong ought to bear the infirmities of the weak, and not to please ourselves."** During my own trial, I experienced people's love and support, yet I remained disciplined in doing everything I could. Every morning, I got out of bed, did my hair and makeup, and acted as though I was well, even when I had to hold onto walls to steady myself. I went to dinners with friends, though I often couldn't keep up with the conversation. Gradually, out of kindness, they would converse among themselves, knowing I couldn't fully participate. I was aware of everything but felt imprisoned within myself, unable to communicate clearly.

When Rex saw me, I was barely able to walk, but I was committed to fulfilling my purpose, for I have learned that faith requires action. **James 2:17** declares, **"Even so faith, if it hath not works, is dead, being alone."** It's easy to encourage others to "believe God," but I had years of building my faith in God's Word, which sustained me even when I was too weak to pray. Faith is powerful and energizing, alive and active, and I was determined to minister as planned. Within a week of Rex's arrival, I began to walk better, though my muscles had deteriorated from inactivity, leaving me physically weak.

As Rex continued to California, I also prepared for my speaking engagement. I had to change planes three times, requiring me to transfer between flights despite my limitations. In the natural, one might not think I could make it, but I held onto faith, trusting that God would strengthen me for the journey. **Philippians 4:13** assured me, **"I can do all things through Christ which strengtheneth me."**

That Friday morning, I left Tulsa at 7:00 a.m., bound for a healing service in California later that night. When I arrived in Dallas, I could barely walk off the plane, but my friend Sharon met me with a cart, helping me get to my next flight. Each step, each leg of the journey, was guided by God's grace. As **2 Corinthians 12:9** says, **"And he said unto me, My grace is sufficient for thee: for my strength is made perfect in weakness."** It was by His strength alone that I persevered, and I am grateful to have witnessed His power working through my weakness.

When we arrived in California, they had a wheelchair waiting for me. I must admit, it felt humbling and even humiliating. Here I was, a healing evangelist, being wheeled through Los Angeles International Airport in a wheelchair. Three women recognized me and asked, "Are you Vicki Jamison?" I answered, "Yes." They looked heartbroken. How could their hero, a healing evangelist, be in a wheelchair? I didn't have the heart to tell them I was on my way to a healing service that very night. It reminded me of **2 Corinthians 4:7**, which says, **"But we have this treasure in earthen vessels, that the excellency of the power may be of God, and not of us."**

Faith without works is dead **(James 2:17),** and I knew I had to put action behind my words. We arrived that

Vicki Jamison Peterson: God's Anointed Vessel

afternoon, and I tried to prepare. Weak and exhausted, I couldn't even stand to fix my hair in the mirror. Without a chair, I used a luggage rack to sit and get ready. When I reached the service, I felt so weak I barely knew my own name. But Rex, Sharon, and the believers there had faith, lifting me up in prayer. I was called to the front, where I was expected to lead. There was no one else to lead worship, so I sang the only song I could remember—*Blessed Assurance*. I had to use what I had, and as we sang, the words came alive in me: "Blessed assurance, Jesus is mine."

From there, I remembered a few other songs, like *He Lives* and *Hallelujah*, and we worshiped. It would have been easier to stay home in bed; it would have been more comfortable to step back from ministry. But I am led, not driven. As **Romans 8:14** says, **"For as many as are led by the Spirit of God, they are the sons of God."** If I had failed to demonstrate the faith I had preached, it would not have changed the truth of faith, but I would have lost the blessing of witnessing its power in my own life.

As I began to call out healings, people experienced the power of God throughout the room. Though I felt detached, barely conscious of the moment, I called out, "Your leg is healed; your arm is healed." Miraculously, people were being touched and healed, and I discovered that the anointing of the Holy Spirit was giving me strength. Slowly, I began to stand with more stability, able to walk across the platform by the end of the service. I even announced to the audience, "Look at how well I am walking!"

We all desire instant and permanent miracles, but God's ways are often a journey rather than a moment. In **Isaiah 40:31**, we are reminded, **"But they that wait upon the Lord shall renew their strength; they shall mount up with wings as eagles; they shall run, and not be weary; and they shall walk, and not faint."** That night, I experienced the sustaining power of God and learned that even in our weakest moments, He is more than enough.

** "Sustained by the Anointing: Embracing Healing and Strength Through Faith"**

I have literally held onto healing moment by moment. Each time, it only gets better. The next night, I led another healing service, and by Sunday morning, I had to be up early for a service in another city. As I entered the church, an overwhelming sense of illness struck me—I felt as though I was dying. The thought kept running through my mind, "I am dying." But faith presses on. I stepped up to the podium as the minister of the gospel, not to succumb to illness, but to proclaim the Word of God. Miraculously, people were healed that morning, and I witnessed more healings than ever before.

That evening, I led another service. The next night, Monday, I led yet another. On Tuesday, while traveling to Los Angeles, a sudden virus struck me, the same flu that was keeping people bedridden for days. We stopped at a motel, and by the next morning, I rose completely

Vicki Jamison Peterson: God's Anointed Vessel

well, untouched by the illness. **Isaiah 53:5** promises, **"But he was wounded for our transgressions, he was bruised for our iniquities: the chastisement of our peace was upon him; and with his stripes, we are healed."** That morning, I led a 10 o'clock healing service, and 70% of the audience experienced healing—a powerful move of God.

As I continued, I discovered that every time I sat or stood in one of my services where the anointing of God was present, I grew stronger. But it required effort; I had to get my body there, even though my body craved rest. We are reminded in **1 Corinthians 9:27, "But I keep under my body, and bring it into subjection."** My spirit wasn't abusing my body, but I was bringing it into alignment with the truth of God's Word. The Word declares in **1 Peter 2:24, "By whose stripes ye were healed."** Saying that alone is powerful, but when coupled with the anointing of the Holy Spirit, we enter a dimension of wholeness and completion.

Many times, as we sit under the anointing, we may not witness dramatic occurrences, yet the Spirit of God is at work in ways we can't always see. It's like sandpaper, smoothing out the rough edges, working on us gently but effectively. As **John 16:13** tells us, **"Howbeit when he, the Spirit of truth, is come, he will guide you into all truth."** When we dwell under the anointing, the Spirit works within us, often in ways we don't understand.

What I don't comprehend is when individuals seeking healing only give God a single chance, attending just one service and, if they don't see an immediate result, deciding not to return. Or those who receive healing but don't return to give glory. **Luke 17:15-17** shows us the importance of gratitude and faithfulness, as only one of the ten lepers returned to thank Jesus. God's power is always present, and one of the most important lessons I've learned through this experience is to remain where the anointing is—stay around it, seek it continually.

It grieves me to see empty seats in the front row, seats that should be filled by those desiring to receive from God. **Psalm 84:10** reminds us, **"For a day in thy courts is better than a thousand."** I encourage everyone to stay close to the anointing, for that's where His Spirit works, healing us and strengthening our faith, day by day.

Do you know how I received the anointing for my ministry? Here's a secret—one I'm eager to share. I was so hungry for God. I didn't desire a ministry, nor did I ask for one. I simply longed for God. I used to sit on the front row at Kenneth Hagin's meetings, simply to feel the power of God. Broken in body, I didn't tell anyone how I felt; I didn't announce that I could feel the power. I just sat there, absorbing it, not knowing then that this anointing would flow into me and prepare me for a ministry of healing.

I would be on the front row every night because I wanted to be close to the anointing. Though it's true that the Spirit moves everywhere, there's something about being near the source of an anointed ministry. **Luke 8:46** shows this truth when Jesus said, **"Somebody hath touched me: for I perceive that virtue is gone out of me."** If Jesus were to be announced as present in the

Vicki Jamison Peterson: God's Anointed Vessel

flesh, everyone would rush to the front to be near Him, not out of guilt but out of a desire to be close to His presence. When God anoints men and women with special gifts, we should be near, not worshiping the individual, but absorbing that tangible anointing of the Holy Spirit.

Returning from that trip, I was strong for two or three days because of that power, yet soon after, I felt myself slipping again. Still, every day, I got up, dressed, and acted as though I was healed, even when it hurt. There were times I wanted to cry from the pain. But faith doesn't quit. **Hebrews 10:23** says**, "Let us hold fast the profession of our faith without wavering; (for he is faithful that promised)."** Even when I didn't feel strong, I clung to that truth.

Some of you may be standing in faith, thinking, "Well, I didn't receive it." But in the spiritual realm, we possess by faith. God gives, and we must take hold of it. **Deuteronomy 1:8** encourages us, **"Behold, I have set the land before you: go in and possess the land."** This promise shows that God may offer, but we are to actively receive. Why did I get sick? Not because God wanted it, but because I didn't apply principles of health in my life. Over time, stress and strain took their toll.

In every season, I have learned to draw near to the anointing, to persevere, and to lean on God's strength, knowing that as we hold fast to His promises, He is faithful to sustain and heal us.

"Renewed by the Anointing: Persevering Through Weakness to Greater Strength and Clarity"

I had worn down my body, pushing it beyond its limits. But as I ministered, the strength of the Spirit would lift me, only to hit walls again afterward. This cycle continued for weeks. Near the end of January, there was a seminar at Rhema Bible School led by Kenneth Hagin. Each night, I intended to go, but something came up—Monday, Tuesday, Wednesday. By Thursday, the Spirit of the Lord stirred urgently within me, saying, "You must go tonight." When my husband came home, I told him, "Carl, we need to go to Rhema tonight." He agreed.

On the way, I was tired of talking about how bad I felt; people grow weary of hearing complaints. **Proverbs 18:21** reminds us, **"Death and life are in the power of the tongue."** Even though every part of my body hurt, I kept my focus. When we arrived, my husband dropped me at the door, and I found a seat near the front. Immersed in the praise and worship, I sensed God's presence profoundly.

That night, Brother Hagin called me down and spoke words that only the Holy Spirit could have revealed. He said, "You can't quit." He ministered about the greater anointing God was preparing me for, a ministry that would bless many. **Jeremiah 29:11** reassures us, **"For I know the thoughts that I think toward you, saith the LORD, thoughts of peace, and not of evil, to give you an expected end."** His words filled me with excitement and renewed purpose, and as I left the building, I realized

Vicki Jamison Peterson: God's Anointed Vessel

I was energized, walking straight, thinking clearly—free from all symptoms.

From the moment I had entered that auditorium, the symptoms had lifted. I was fully under the anointing of the Holy Spirit. Yet, by the next afternoon, the symptoms tried to return. Satan would have loved for me to accept defeat, but I had learned a valuable truth: **"Resist the devil, and he will flee from you" (James 4:7).** The Spirit showed me that through His Word, and by not surrendering, I could overcome.

I've realized it's not easy—it takes intentional faith and perseverance. As **Galatians 6:9** encourages, **"And let us not be weary in well doing: for in due season we shall reap, if we faint not."** Many might choose to accept their circumstances, knowing they'll go to heaven, but I plan to live fully here, not in a nursing home or hindered by limitations. The Lord has sharpened my mind, making me more articulate and clearer than ever before.

The knowledge of the Spirit I now receive surpasses anything I've understood in my life. Truly, **"The entrance of thy words giveth light; it giveth understanding unto the simple" (Psalm 119:130).** His anointing is teaching me new things, filling me with strength, clarity, and a greater understanding of His purposes.

**"Unveiling Divine Mysteries: Embracing the

Revelation and Knowledge of God"**

For the Lord God is a great God, and He will yet reveal unto His people the deepest and most intimate secrets of knowledge that have been kept since the beginning of time. As **Psalm 95:3** declares, ****"For the LORD is a great God, and a great King above all gods."****

You have come to an hour of the revealing of Christ. We are in a time when the mysteries are going to be made known because Christ is a mystery, and His Church is a mystery. As the Apostle Paul wrote **in Colossians 1:26-27, **"Even the mystery which hath been hid from ages and from generations, but now is made manifest to his saints: To whom God would make known what is the riches of the glory of this mystery among the Gentiles; which is Christ in you, the hope of glory."****

But the world is going to see the veil taken back, and the heart of the Father is going to be revealed. The heart of the Father is wholeness—body, soul, and spirit. Great knowledge is going to be imparted unto His children. The world will look and say, "Where have they received this? Where did they get this authority? And where did they get this hidden knowledge?" As it is written in **Matthew 13:11, **"He answered and said unto them, Because it is given unto you to know the mysteries of the kingdom of heaven, but to them it is not given."****

But it shall be an amazing fact that shall break upon the mind. Know you not that even before the fall, Adam was endowed with great knowledge? Did he not have dominion over all things? Did he not name all of creation? Did he not have control over all living things? **Genesis 1:28** affirms this: ****"And God blessed them, and God said unto them, Be fruitful, and multiply, and replenish the earth, and subdue it: and have dominion over the fish of the sea, and over the fowl of the air, and over every living thing that moveth upon the earth."****

You will see a full restoration in the Church of the knowledge of the children of the living God. For the Holy Ghost is creation in your mind and shall become what God wants it to become, and the knowledge of the Lord shall fill the earth. **Habakkuk 2:14** prophesies, ****"For the earth shall be filled with the knowledge of the glory of the LORD, as the waters cover the sea."**** And you are the Church to be filled with that knowledge.

So there are hidden mysteries—we've talked about them for years—but we're at the time of the uncovering of the hidden mysteries in every area: spiritually, scientifically, medically. Jesus said in **Mark 4:22, **"For there is nothing hid, which shall not be manifested; neither was any thing kept secret, but that it should come abroad."****

And there are some things that we need to really be keyed in on in prayer, and keen on in prayer. Specifically, Ephesians, the first chapter, the 17th verse through the 22nd—for revelation knowledge. Pray for yourself, for your household, for those around you, for people who are in positions of authority, because revelation knowledge is flowing; discoveries are being made spiritually. We're learning principles that are working.

Ephesians 1:17-22 says, **"**That the God of our Lord Jesus Christ, the Father of glory, may give unto you the spirit of wisdom and revelation in the knowledge of him: The eyes of your understanding being enlightened; that ye may know what is the hope of his calling, and what the riches of the glory of his inheritance in the saints, And what is the exceeding greatness of his power to us-ward who believe, according to the working of his mighty power, Which he wrought in Christ, when he raised him from the dead, and set him at his own right hand in the heavenly places, Far above all principality, and power, and might, and dominion, and every name that is named, not only in this world, but also in that which is to come: And hath put all things under his feet, and gave him to be the head over all things to the church."****

There are things that we know, that we've learned, that we can't yet tell because people can't comprehend them. Some of them are not really ready for them, see? And if you'd share some of them, they'd say, "Oh, they're so crazy. They're off in left field." So what you have to do is keep giving milk. As Paul wrote **in 1 Corinthians 3:1-2, **"And I, brethren, could not speak unto you as unto spiritual, but as unto carnal, even as unto babes in Christ. I have fed you with milk, and not with meat: for hitherto ye were not able to bear it, neither yet now are ye able."****

Vicki Jamison Peterson: God's Anointed Vessel

Let us continue to seek the Lord, embracing the knowledge and revelation He is imparting in these times. May we grow in understanding and be vessels for His glory.

DR MICAEL H YEAGER
AUTHORS SUPERNATURAL EXPERIENCE

Stabbed in the Face with a knife Multiple Times by a demon possessed women!

While I was in Anchorage, Alaska, it was quickened in my heart to stop at a small full gospel church that I used to visit. The Neighborhood Full Gospel Church. Now, It just so happened that an evangelist I had known while I was in the Navy on Adak, Alaska, was there. We spent some time reminiscing about what had happened while we were in Adak. (1977)

He shared how the Lord had laid upon his heart to go to Pennsylvania to open an evangelistic outreach center in a town called Mount Union, Pennsylvania. He invited me to go to Pennsylvania with him and his wife to open this evangelistic outreach.

I perceived in my heart I needed to go with them. I planned to fly back to Wisconsin where he and his wife would pick me up as they went through. However, before

I left Alaska the spirit of God had one more assignment for me: a precious demon possessed woman needed to be set free.

One Sunday we decided to attend a small church along the road to Fairbanks. I was the first to enter this little, old, rustic church. When I went through the sanctuary doors, I immediately noticed a strange, little, elderly, lady across from me - sitting in the pews.

She turned her head and stared right at me with the strangest look I had ever seen. I could sense immediately there was something demonic about her. Out of the blue, this little old lady jumped up, got out of the pew, and ran out of the church. At that moment I perceived that God wanted me to go and cast the devils out of her.

When the service was over, I asked the pastor who that elderly lady was. He said she was not a member of his church, but she came once in a great while. He also told me that she lived with her husband in a run-down house on a dirt road. I asked him if it would be okay to go and see her. (I knew in my heart that God had sent me there to help bring deliverance) He said he had no problems with this, especially since she wasn't a part of his church.

We followed the directions the pastor gave us, and when we arrived at the house it was exactly as the pastor had described it to us. It was run-down, and the yard was overflowing with old furniture and household items. It reminded me of the TV show "Sanford and Son" - but it probably had ten-times more junk in the yard! I do not know how the old couple survived the winters in Alaska in such a poorly-built house.

Vicki Jamison Peterson: God's Anointed Vessel

As we got out of the car, a little old man met us outside. It was her husband. He was thanking God as he walked toward us, and said he knew we were men of God, and that we had been sent by the Lord to help his poor, tormented wife. That God had heard his many years of prayer. Can you imagine here was a man who had been crying out to God for over forty years for God to send someone to help him. Yet in all these years there was no help. God had to send a 21-year-old kid who had only been saved for two years.

Ezekiel 22:30 (KJV). "And I sought for a man among them, that should make up the hedge, and stand in the gap before me for the land, that I should not destroy it: but I found none."

The husband informed us that his wife was in their summer kitchen. So, we walked up to the house, having to go down the twisting and cluttered junk-filled path. We entered the summer kitchen, which was a small block building through a screen door. When we entered the kitchen, we could see his wife over at a large utility sink. Her back was to us, but we could see she was peeling carrots over her kitchen sink ... with a very large, scary-looking, butchers knife!

As I stood there, looking at the back of her head, I began to speak to her about Jesus. Out of the blue, she turned her head like it was on a swivel to look at me. I could hardly believe my eyes! It was like I was watching a horror movie! This little lady's eyes were glowing red on her swiveled head.

I rubbed my eyes at that moment; thinking that maybe I

imagined this. No ... her head had swiveled - without her body moving - and her eyes were glowing red. Fear immediately filled my heart as she looked at me with the big knife ... a butcher's knife ... in her hand. Immediately, I came against the spirit of fear in my heart by quoting the holy Scriptures: **"For God hath not given me the spirit of fear; but of power, and of love, and of a sound mind" 2 Timothy 1:7.** I began to share with her about Jesus Christ.

The next thing I knew she was coming right at me faster than humanly possible - with her knife - as if she was filled with great rage. The knife was still in her right hand when she spun around and came at me. She leapt through the air onto me, wrapping her small skinny legs around my waist, like a monkey on a psalm tree. How in the world she was able to do this - I do not know?! The next thing I knew, she was lifting her right hand and hitting me in the face, very hard, multiple times. I could feel the pressure of her hitting me on the left side of my face. I felt her repeated hits as her fist slammed into me. (At least I thought it was her fist) As she was hitting me in the face, out of my mouth came: "In the Name of Jesus!"

The minute I came against this attack "In The Name of Jesus" she was ripped off of me; picked up by an invisible power and flung across the room about 10-feet or more. She slammed very hard against the bare block wall of her kitchen, and slipped down to the floor. Amazingly when she hit the wall, she was not hurt! I went over to her, continuing to cast the demons out of her In the Name of Jesus. Once I perceived that she was free, and in her right mind, I asked her how she had become

Vicki Jamison Peterson: God's Anointed Vessel

demon possessed? She told us her terrible story.

Her uncle had repeatedly molested and raped her when she was a very young girl. She thought she was free from him when he got sick and died. But then he began to visit her from the dead, continuing to molest and rape her at night.

To her, it was physical and real. She did not know it was a familiar spirit disguised as her uncle. This had probably gone on for over fifty years! I led her to the Lord and into the baptism of the Holy Ghost. Sweet, beautiful peace came upon her, completely changing her countenance. I then led her husband to the Lord and into the baptism of the Spirit.

She was a brand-new person in Christ, finally free - after almost sixty years of torment. She and her husband began to go to church with us - until I left Alaska. I remember that we took them to see the Davis family at a local church, visiting Alaska on a missionary trip.

Years later, the evangelist who visited this lady with me, heard me retelling the story at a church; about how the woman kept punching me forcefully with her right hand. At the end of the service, he came and informed me that I was not telling the story correctly. I wondered if he thought I was exaggerating. He said that he was standing behind me when she ran at me and jumped on top of me and began to hit me with her right fist.

But he informed me, it wasn't her hand she was slapping me with … she still had the large butchers knife in her hand; and he saw her stabbing me in the face with this knife. Repeatedly!! He said he expected there to be a massive pool of blood with my face all tore up. He said he knew that I was a dead man, because nobody could survive being stabbed in the face repeatedly, with a large butcher knife.

He expected to see nothing but blood, but instead of seeing my blood everywhere, he saw that there was not even one mark on my face where the knife was hitting me. I did feel something hit my face repeatedly, but I thought it was her hand! Instead, it was her knife, and it could not pierce my skin! Thank God for His love, His mercy, and His Supernatural Divine Protection.

Luke 10:19 Behold, I give unto you power to tread on serpents and scorpions, and over all the power of the enemy: and nothing shall by any means hurt you.

I am convinced that if I had not been walking with God in His holiness and obedience, the devil in that little old lady would have stabbed me to death. I was living the life of a one percenter totally yielded to God! Many people in the body of Christ are trying to deal with demonic powers when they are out of the Father's will.

When we are moving in the Holy Ghost, obedience, and absolute love for Jesus Christ - there is no power in hell that can hurt us!

My God hath sent his angel, and hath shut the lion's mouths, that they have not hurt me: forasmuch as before him innocence was found in me; and also before thee, O king, have I done no hurt (Daniel 6:22).

CHAPTER FOUR

"Embracing Divine Knowledge: Preparing for Greater Works Through the Anointing"

But there is more—not to try to seem super mysterious—but there is knowledge that is available that will help us in the areas of healing that is simply superb. I know I will be operating in this within the next two years. But I have another year—the Lord told me—of studying. I have a year of studying. My next year is to study. I'll be ministering, but I'll be studying. But watch out after a year because, you see, the greater miracles will then begin to be released. I see miracles until then, but after that, the greater works are going to begin to unfold very miraculously.

Now, there's a timing for everything, but God wants us to come into His perfect will. And right now, I'm going to ask you: If you desire more knowledge of the anointing and the gifts of the Spirit—if you want to know more from the Lord, if you'd like Him to reveal the Word to you—just ask in faith believing, at the same time put action to your prays.

Now, Father, You said, **"Ask, and it shall be given you"** (Matthew 7:7, KJV). And in the name of Jesus, with my heart open. My Lord, I come before You as Your son *or* daughter, available, open to study, to learn, to grow. You may speak to me in any way You choose. I am are open to any and everything.

And You said that **"there is nothing hid, which shall not be manifested"** (Mark 4:22, KJV). So, reveal the hidden things, Father. Reveal the hidden things that I need to know in life, in my businesses, that will bring out truth—the hidden things that I need to know to help me to come into the nature of Christ in my life. Reveal those hidden things that I might come into fullness and knowledge and strength—the power of the gifts of the Spirit—that we would flow within the gifts that the Spirit would use us me, and that we would be available, and that wisdom would watch over us. Wisdom would guard us.

In Jesus' name we say, Amen.

"Embracing the Ministry of Revival: A Journey of Faith and Anointing"

Father, this is Your time, and we confess that the Greater One is within us than he that is in the world. As it is

Vicki Jamison Peterson: God's Anointed Vessel

written in **1 John 4:4** (KJV): *"Ye are of God, little children, and have overcome them: because greater is he that is in you, than he that is in the world."* Because the Greater One abides within us, I confess that You will cause my thoughts to become agreeable with Your thoughts.

Let the words of my mouth and the meditation of my heart be acceptable in Thy sight. As **Psalm 19:14** (KJV) declares: *"Let the words of my mouth, and the meditation of my heart, be acceptable in thy sight, O LORD, my strength, and my redeemer."* Let my tongue be as the pen of a ready writer. According to **Psalm 45:1** (KJV): *"My heart is inditing a good matter: I speak of the things which I have made touching the king: my tongue is the pen of a ready writer."*

And I thank You, Father, that it is possible because You are the One who brings it to pass, in Jesus' wonderful name.

As **Philippians 2:9-11** (KJV) reminds us: *"Wherefore God also hath highly exalted him, and given him a name which is above every name: That at the name of Jesus every knee should bow, of things in heaven, and things in earth, and things under the earth; And that every tongue should confess that Jesus Christ is Lord, to the glory of God the Father."*

I can be fervent when it comes to teaching faith. Just take

my word for it—will you do that? I may touch on a few challenging points, but I'll bring you back into the positive, for I want to share with you as a new person in the ministry, now stepping into a new dimension and aspect that is developing—the ministry of revival.

Do not be surprised at what God asks you to give. But remember this: God is your source, the one who supplies all your needs. As **Philippians 4:19** (KJV) assures us, *"But my God shall supply all your need according to his riches in glory by Christ Jesus."* He desires us to be a channel, an open vessel for His blessings to flow through. That's why we're in ministry—not merely to receive, but to give.

When He asked if we would give a possession, we knew the Word of God works when it is activated. I turned to **Luke 6:38**, which declares, *"Give, and it shall be given unto you; good measure, pressed down, and shaken together, and running over, shall men give into your bosom."* This promise applies to every area of life: spiritually, physically, and materially. Often, people focus on the material blessing first, but as we mature in Christ, we understand that God's principles of giving encompass every dimension of life.

For example, when Fern and Phil Halverson felt the Lord's call to give more to His work, God challenged them: *"Give according to what you want to receive."* Instead of giving only a tenth of their income, they began giving as though their income level was already increased. And as they gave in faith, not only did their

Vicki Jamison Peterson: God's Anointed Vessel

income grow, but the gifts of the Holy Spirit began to operate powerfully in their lives. **2 Corinthians 9:6** emphasizes, *"He which soweth sparingly shall reap also sparingly; and he which soweth bountifully shall reap also bountifully."*

I believe we should get every benefit we can from the Word of God. He wants us to be blessed on every level—physically, spiritually, materially, and financially. In **3 John 1:2**, we read, *"Beloved, I wish above all things that thou mayest prosper and be in health, even as thy soul prospereth."* This blessing is on three dimensions, showing us that God's desire is for complete wholeness and prosperity.

Giving is vital, but we must also release our faith when we give. Here's what I've learned to do: I pray, "Father, because I have given, Your Word says it will be given unto me. I am giving, and I am confessing that because I am a doer of the Word, not a hearer only (**James 1:22**), it shall be given unto me—good measure, pressed down, shaken together, and running over." **Proverbs 3:9-10** also reminds us, *"Honour the LORD with thy substance, and with the firstfruits of all thine increase: So shall thy barns be filled with plenty, and thy presses shall burst out with new wine."*

When we pray this way, we open ourselves to the storehouse of God's blessings. However, the moment we become selfish or inward-focused, the flow of blessings can slow down, like a faucet shutting off. When God asked me to give a treasured possession to another ministry, I responded, "Father, I'm planting this seed for a greater outpouring of the Holy Spirit in our ministry." **Galatians 6:7** confirms, *"Be not deceived; God is not mocked: for whatsoever a man soweth, that shall he also reap."*

God opened doors for me in ministry through three-day teaching sessions and preaching engagements—the "charismatic glamour circuit." While that path is good, I longed for something more, something deeper—a true, Holy Ghost outpouring of the Spirit. **Joel 2:28** promises, *"And it shall come to pass afterward, that I will pour out my spirit upon all flesh."* This hunger for revival fuels my giving and my dedication to serve as a willing channel for God's work.

Let us continue to give, not only to receive but to become vessels through which God's blessings and Spirit can flow into the world.

** "Reviving the Church: The Power of the Holy Spirit in Transformational Revival"**

They used to call them revivals, when people would fall under the power of God, slain in the Spirit for hours, where they would see Jesus, where lives were changed and thrust into new spiritual dimensions. These were times when we sought God's power to transform humanity in a profound way. And we are living in that

Vicki Jamison Peterson: God's Anointed Vessel

day, aren't we? But I desired this in my ministry as well.

As I began to confess the promises of God after we had given, the very first thing that happened was a revival in New Orleans for three days of services. On the third night, a man who was bent over, crippled, unable to stand, was healed. When I declared, *"Be healed in the name of Jesus!"* he stretched forth his body, and the Lord straightened him like an arrow. The audience was astonished, as they witnessed the power of God. **Psalm 77:14** reminds us, *"**Thou art the God that doest wonders: thou hast declared thy strength among the people.**"*

God was showing His power to reach every heart, every denomination. We have seen people from all walks, even a former Mormon who testified to receiving Jesus as his Savior and being baptized in the Holy Spirit. God isn't limited by labels—He has reached into places of darkness, even among those in Satanic worship, bringing them to know Jesus. It is the open, hungry heart that He draws to Himself. **John 6:44** declares, *"**No man can come to me, except the Father which hath sent me draw him.**"*

It is amazing to see the direction God has taken, guiding me into a ministry of revival within the Assemblies of God. At first, I was surprised. With my background, I didn't expect it, yet God knows where our personality and ministry will fit best. **Proverbs 3:5-6** encourages us to, *"**Trust in the LORD with all thine heart; and lean not unto thine own understanding. In**

all thy ways acknowledge him, and he shall direct thy paths." * He has known the path for each of us.

Now, I want to turn to **Romans 8:26-27** to see how the Holy Spirit works in intercession. **Romans 8:26-27 (Amplified) says, *"So too the Holy Spirit comes to our aid and bears us up in our weakness; for we do not know what prayer to offer nor how to offer it worthily as we ought, but the Spirit Himself goes to meet our supplication and pleads in our behalf with unspeakable yearnings and groanings too deep for utterance. And He who searches the hearts of men knows what is in the mind of the Spirit, because the Spirit intercedes and pleads before God on behalf of the saints according to and in harmony with God's will."***

This scripture brings me into a new appreciation for the work of the Holy Spirit. Sometimes we treat the Holy Spirit as if He's at our disposal, but He is the gentle, brooding presence, hovering over the body of Christ, as **Genesis 1:2** portrays Him *"moving upon the face of the waters."* Through this move of revival, the Lord has opened my eyes to a dimension of compassion I hadn't fully understood before.

Phil Halverson, after he and Fern began giving to the Kingdom of God, saw a release of the Holy Spirit's gifts, especially in intercession. God desires to reveal His heart to us and through us, transforming lives through the depth and power of His Spirit. We are called to yield to the Holy Spirit, to be used in God's mighty work of

Vicki Jamison Peterson: God's Anointed Vessel

revival, as He fills us with compassion and empowers us to reach a broken world with His love and truth.

"Guided by the Spirit: The Power of Intercession and Divine Revelation"

I love praying with Fern and Phil, as we listen to Phil praying in tongues and then hear him give the interpretation in English. Often, the Holy Spirit speaks words Phil doesn't know, names he's unfamiliar with, locations he hasn't been to, and situations beyond his comprehension. Through this intercession, the Spirit broods over people's lives, and I've stood in awe, feeling deeply moved. **Romans 8:26** reminds us, *"Likewise the Spirit also helpeth our infirmities: for we know not what we should pray for as we ought: but the Spirit itself maketh intercession for us with groanings which cannot be uttered."*

To think that the Holy Spirit is interceding over your life even now, caring for every little detail, is both humbling and comforting. The Spirit works through those who yield to the call of intercession. Phil Halverson, led by the Holy Spirit, felt called to New Orleans.

That revival in New Orleans was my first time speaking for more than three days straight, and I felt far from prepared. But when God saw I wasn't ready to stand alone, He sent people to hold my hands in prayer. **Exodus 17:12** illustrates this beautifully, *"But

Moses' hands were heavy; and they took a stone, and put it under him, and he sat thereon; and Aaron and Hur stayed up his hands, the one on the one side, and the other on the other side; and his hands were steady until the going down of the sun."* It's a comfort to know that when we act in faith and trust in God, He faithfully provides the support we need.

Phil, why don't you share how you were led to New Orleans? Before we even arrived, the Spirit revealed to him specific details about the building and the people he would meet.

As I prayed, the Lord revealed to Fern and me that we should join the Jamison's in South Bend. But just before we left Minneapolis, the Holy Spirit revealed to me through a word of knowledge that they were no longer in South Bend. I told Fern to trace their location, and she discovered that they were now in New Orleans. Wes confirmed they'd be there for a few more days, so we booked our flight.

Before we went, I'd been interceding for the Assemblies of God and praying earnestly for the revival in New Orleans. As we flew over the city for the first time, I encountered a profound experience of spiritual warfare. **Ephesians 6:12** warns us, ***"For we wrestle not against flesh and blood, but against principalities, against powers, against the rulers of the darkness of this world, against spiritual wickedness in high places."*** I felt the evil presence in the atmosphere but also sensed the Lord filling my heart and strengthening

Vicki Jamison Peterson: God's Anointed Vessel

my spirit.

Through the power of intercession and the revelation of the Holy Spirit, we have witnessed lives changed, strongholds broken, and the love of God poured out. The Spirit equips those willing to yield, bringing about divine alignment with God's will and empowering us to confront spiritual forces with confidence and strength.

"Empowered by the Spirit: Standing Firm in Faith and Spiritual Authority"

As we left New Orleans, I witnessed the Lord's powerful work there, and although I won't go into every detail, one experience stood out. As our plane took off, the pilot mentioned what a beautiful day it was, saying it would be a smooth flight to Dallas. But within minutes, I felt led to pray in the Spirit, rebuking the work of Satan. Suddenly, the plane began to shake violently, lights flashing with the "fasten your seatbelt" warning. I prayed, and the turbulence ceased. Once again, I sensed the darkness that we had confronted in New Orleans, knowing we had come against that power in the mighty name of Jesus. **Philippians 2:10** reminds us, *"**That at the name of Jesus every knee should bow, of things in heaven, and things in earth, and things under the earth.**"*

I believe the Holy Spirit is preparing to demonstrate His power among us as we pray together, not just to teach, but to actively participate in the work of God, for we are

His body. **1 Corinthians 12:27** says, *"Now ye are the body of Christ, and members in particular."* Let us enter into prayer with a unified heart.

Ephesians 6:10-11 exhorts us, *"Finally, my brethren, be strong in the Lord, and in the power of his might. Put on the whole armour of God, that ye may be able to stand against the wiles of the devil."* The Spirit empowers us to go forth, carrying His Word to the world, bringing life, healing, and the power of the Holy Spirit.

Prayer: Obey, yes, for we obey Thy voice, O Lord. We come, Father, to do Thy will, and with You there are no minimums. There are no limits in Christ Jesus. Of that abundance, Father, we receive—yes, we receive the fullness of what Thou has provided, from Thy throne of grace. Our hearts are open to receive what You will have for us this day. **Ephesians 3:20** (KJV) reminds us, *"Now unto him that is able to do exceeding abundantly above all that we ask or think, according to the power that worketh in us."* Amen.

Blessed Lord and Savior, precious Lord and Savior, we thank You, Father. We praise You, Lord Jesus. We worship You. Thank You, Father, that this class is sent with purpose, destined for the four corners of the earth. **Matthew 28:19** calls us to, *"Go ye therefore, and teach all nations,"* and Lord, we thank You for this commission. Right now, we receive Your provision—spiritual, financial, and material—for each one here. I thank You for propelling these laborers into the harvest

Vicki Jamison Peterson: God's Anointed Vessel

field. Father, I lift up those who will go to Africa, to rural America, to India, to Alaska, to Canada, to South and Central America. Through these vessels, Father, I believe You will reach the world.

Romans 2:11 assures us, *"For there is no respect of persons with God."* What You have done for me, You will do for each of them. Glory to Your name, Lord! We worship You, Jesus. Precious Lord, we lift up our hearts and voices to You. Let Your gentle rain fall upon us by the Spirit of God. Precious, wonderful Jesus! **Psalm 72:6** declares, *"He shall come down like rain upon the mown grass: as showers that water the earth."* Thank You, Lord, for Your presence, refreshing our spirits.

Psalm 103:2-3 reminds us, *"Bless the LORD, O my soul, and forget not all his benefits: Who forgiveth all thine iniquities; who healeth all thy diseases."* Thank You, Lord, for Your healing power and for the abundant blessings that You pour upon us, that we may walk in health, strength, and purpose for Your glory.

"Healing Through the Holy Spirit: A Testimony of Miracles and Divine Intercession"

Psalm 103:3 (KJV) declares, *"Who forgiveth all thine iniquities; who healeth all thy diseases."* **Words of knowledge:** Excruciating pain in the back of the throat—healed, cleansed, and clear. Give God the praise and glory for His healing touch!

Arthritis in the hand, with calcium deposits in the joints, is being healed. The Spirit of the Lord is removing that, and your hands are whole in Jesus' name. **Mark 16:18** promises, *"They shall lay hands on the sick, and they shall recover."*

Another healing—a respiratory condition is being touched by the Spirit. Take a deep breath; the lungs are healed. Pressure in the lungs, unrelated to an infection but connected to an old affliction, is leaving as your lungs are restored by the power of the Holy Spirit. Give God the glory for what is happening in your body at this very moment! **Isaiah 53:5** reminds us, *"And with his stripes we are healed."* You are healed, and isn't it wonderful to have the Holy Spirit ministering healing among us?

The Spirit of the Lord intercedes on our behalf before we enter revivals, whispering names of streets, locations, and people we will meet—praying for them even before we arrive. **Romans 8:26** (KJV) says, *"Likewise the Spirit also helpeth our infirmities: for we know not what we should pray for as we ought: but the Spirit itself maketh intercession for us with groanings which cannot be uttered."*

Recently, we ministered at the PTL Network, focusing solely on healing, showing the world what God is doing and will do through signs and wonders. When they witness God's works, they become open to His Word. During our time there, God reminded us of His love and

Vicki Jamison Peterson: God's Anointed Vessel

provision, placing us in a mansion called "The Mansion" and arriving by limousine. **Psalm 23:1** says, *"The LORD is my shepherd; I shall not want."* He is faithful to provide both our needs and our comforts.

Let us give thanks for the power and love of the Holy Spirit, who heals, intercedes, and reveals His glory among us.

"Divine Appointments: How the Holy Spirit Leads and Intercedes for His People"

Brother Phil had been interceding since October, long before we even knew about the need. We would gather together in prayer, and he would intercede, mentioning "the mansion and the limousine," even before we knew where we were headed. When we arrived and saw the mansion and the limousine waiting, it became clear that God was preparing the way long before we ever arrived. **Jeremiah 33:3** **(KJV)** promises, *"Call unto me, and I will answer thee, and shew thee great and mighty things, which thou knowest not."*

Just before we arrived, Phil was led by the Holy Spirit to pray specifically for a man named Richard. For almost a year, the network had been looking for someone to fill a vacancy as head of all their counselors. That evening, I ministered to the counselors, and Jim Bakker's assistant, Jim Moss, attended in his place. Jim Moss shared, "Something exciting happened just as I was about to leave. We can't announce who it is yet, but we've found the man to head our counselors."

The next day, as we prepared for a live broadcast, I felt restricted and boxed in by the typical television routine. I wasn't called to entertain, but to minister, and I felt an urgency to break out of the routine. As I considered stepping back, Jim Bakker looked over and said, "Feel free to do anything you want." That was all I needed to hear. I leaped up from my seat and said, "Praise the Lord!" **2 Corinthians 3:17** (KJV) affirms, *"Where the Spirit of the Lord is, there is liberty."*

For the next two hours, instead of ministering solely to the audience, we ministered to all of the employees. The Holy Spirit moved mightily, from the third floor to the basement, bringing people to their knees in tears, dedicating their lives, and releasing prophetic words. God had planned that day not only to bless the viewers but also to touch the staff. **Acts 2:17** reminds us, *"And it shall come to pass in the last days, saith God, I will pour out of my Spirit upon all flesh."*

Jim later shared that he'd been searching across America to find someone to head their counseling team, only to realize that Richard—who had been there all along—was the one God had chosen. While Phil had been interceding for Richard, whom he had never met, God was orchestrating the pieces into place. This reminds us that God knows our names and our needs. **Isaiah 49:16** (KJV) assures us, *"Behold, I have graven thee upon the palms of my hands."*

Vicki Jamison Peterson: God's Anointed Vessel

Doesn't it amaze you that God sees every detail and knows our names? He works in ways beyond our understanding, and His Spirit intercedes, setting up divine appointments that lead us into His perfect will.

"Experiencing the Move of the Spirit: Lessons from Salem, Ohio"

In Salem, Ohio, we were blessed to witness the glory of the Lord each night at an Assemblies of God church. Here's a pattern I've noticed that the Holy Spirit establishes in these moves: many believers in this denomination hold to the idea of the Holy Spirit, but some have yet to experience His presence deeply. For some, it's been more a matter of the head than the heart. **Proverbs 3:5** **(KJV)** reminds us, *"***Trust in the LORD with all thine heart; and lean not unto thine own understanding.**"* Just like my grandparents, many of them believe—if Grandpa prayed over the car, they believed. Yet some doubt miracles can happen to them personally.

In ministry, it's crucial to connect with people where they are and understand how they think. **1 Corinthians 9:22** says, *"***I am made all things to all men, that I might by all means save some.**"* When entering a mission field, we must rely on the Holy Spirit, not a preplanned agenda, adapting to the Spirit's flow like logs drifting down a river. This allows God's presence to move freely.

So, on our first night in Salem, the Holy Spirit began to show His power through signs and wonders. The attendees came with questions, observing this unusual woman evangelist. As the night progressed, I noticed an interesting pattern: the Holy Spirit often starts by healing someone close to the pastor—usually a wife or child—making the reality of God's power undeniable for them. When they witness the miraculous firsthand, they acknowledge, "This is real!" **Psalm 77:14** assures us, *"Thou art the God that doest wonders: thou hast declared thy strength among the people."*

Next, the Holy Spirit moves through the gifts of healing and words of knowledge. People in the congregation are healed, some by their faith and others by God's mercy. **1 Corinthians 12:9** tells us, *"To another faith by the same Spirit; to another the gifts of healing by the same Spirit."* Even chronic complainers who may have doubted for years experience God's healing, revealing His power to the church as a sign that He is still at work.

Teaching people to worship is essential but requires patience and gentleness. True worship goes beyond praise; it's the highest form of connection with God. But you can't force people into worship; it's about leading by example. **Psalm 95:6** calls us to, *"O come, let us worship and bow down: let us kneel before the LORD our maker."*

Vicki Jamison Peterson: God's Anointed Vessel

So, I don't demand praise; instead, I simply close my eyes and invite them to "sing in the Spirit." Initially, it's quiet, as many are unsure about singing in tongues. I guide them gently, saying, "Just speak in your prayer language and let it take a melody." I encourage those without a prayer language to say, "Hallelujah," softly. Soon, one or two begin, often timidly, but then the Spirit of worship grows. In time, voices lift, hearts open, and God's presence fills the room.

Psalm 22:3 says, *"But thou art holy, O thou that inhabitest the praises of Israel."* As we yield to the Spirit, worship becomes a powerful force, leading the congregation into deeper encounters with God's glory.

DR MICAEL H YEAGER
AUTHORS SUPERNATURAL EXPERIENCE

"Raising the Dead at Cracker Barrel: The Power of Christ's Compassion"

It was a chilly November morning in 2016 when my wife suggested we have breakfast at Cracker Barrel. This wasn't our usual spot unless Joanna and Randy Herndon—dear friends of ours—were visiting. Still, I agreed, and we set off for the restaurant, about a 20-minute drive from our church in Gettysburg, Pennsylvania.

We arrived around 10 AM, and after being seated, my wife and I began discussing how good God had been to us. Our food arrived, and we held hands, thanking God for His blessings and guidance in our lives. It was a peaceful, leisurely meal, just the two of us enjoying each other's company. But then, something happened.

Out of nowhere, two waitresses began urgently walking through the restaurant, calling out for a doctor or nurse. The look on their faces told us something serious was happening. Normally, I would've been on my feet, ready to help. This wasn't the first time I had encountered an emergency like this. Years ago, I was in a Lowe's store with my family when a cashier suffered an epileptic seizure. I remember running over, telling them I was a doctor—not a medical doctor, but a Ph.D. in biblical theology—and quietly taking authority over the situation. I laid hands on the girl and commanded the seizure to stop in the name of Jesus. She immediately stood up, healed by the power of God.

But this time at Cracker Barrel, I felt no urgency. It was strange, almost as if I was being told to wait. My wife and I continued talking, finishing our meal without rushing. It wasn't until about 10 minutes later that we got up to leave. As we approached the entrance, we noticed a small crowd had gathered. Something drew us closer.

In the middle of the group was a woman lying completely still on the hardwood floor. She appeared to be in her late 60s, and there was an eerie silence as people stood around her. The weight of the situation hit me immediately, and the compassion of God surged

Vicki Jamison Peterson: God's Anointed Vessel

through my heart. In that moment, I felt as if this woman were someone I knew deeply, someone who mattered to me personally like my mom. That's how the Holy Spirit works—He floods your heart with divine love and moves you to act.

I gently made my way through the crowd, telling them I was a local pastor and wanted to help. They stepped aside, allowing me to kneel beside the woman. A nurse was already there, holding the woman's hand and checking for a pulse. I placed my hand on the woman's cheek—it was ice cold.

I've learned over the years that you don't need to shout or make a scene to see God move. Jesus said, *"**They that know their God shall be strong, and do exploits"*** (Daniel 11:32, KJV). Quietly, with tears in my eyes, I prayed a simple prayer in Jesus' name. I commanded the spirit of infirmity to leave and began speaking life over her.

As I prayed, the nurse suddenly exclaimed, "She has a pulse and she had died!" I realized then that the woman had lost her pulse before I arrived, but now, life was returning. I kept my hand on her cheek, continuing to pray softly. Soon after, the woman began to stir. She lifted her hand and gently squeezed mine. I knew at that moment my work was done. The Spirit of Christ had touched her, raising her from the dead.

There were no fireworks, no loud declarations—just the quiet, gentle movement of God's power. Jesus had breathed life back into her, and most of the crowd didn't even realize what had happened.

I stood up, and my wife, who had been patiently waiting, joined me. We walked out of the restaurant just as an ambulance was pulling into the parking lot, its lights flashing. As we got into our car, we took a moment to thank God for His faithfulness and the authority we have in the name of Jesus.

That day was a reminder of the quiet power of Christ's compassion. The love of God, poured out in those moments of obedience, has the power to raise the dead, heal the sick, and transform lives. There was no fanfare—just a simple, heartfelt prayer in the name of Jesus, and a life was restored.

We are called to walk in that love, to surrender to it, and to allow the Holy Spirit to work through us. Whether in a quiet moment at a Cracker Barrel or a more public situation, the love of God is always ready to move, if we're willing to listen and act in faith.

CHAPTER FIVE
"Leading in Worship: Guiding Hearts to the Throne of God"

Psalm 150:6 (KJV) declares, *"Let everything that hath breath praise the LORD. Praise ye the LORD."* When we enter into worship with a melody, it eases the heart and removes fear. People may hesitate if they feel pressured, but when we guide them gently, they're more open to the Spirit's flow. As Paul said in **1 Corinthians 14:15**, *"I will sing with the spirit, and I will sing with the understanding also."* This balance allows people to worship freely.

True worship doesn't require theatrics; you can be "supernaturally natural and naturally supernatural." Isn't that a wonderful thought? When we're led by the Holy Spirit, we don't have to shout or use an exaggerated voice to manifest His power. The anointing of the Spirit speaks for itself. **Zechariah 4:6** affirms, *"Not by might, nor by power, but by my spirit, saith the LORD of hosts."* Whether soft or loud, it's the Spirit that empowers, and we lead others by example in worship.

I've been in services where worship was over-talked, with too much time spent convincing people to praise. It's important not to talk the anointing away. **Psalm 95:6** reminds us, *"O come, let us worship and bow down: let us kneel before the LORD our maker."* We can't force it; we just do it, inviting others to join. Often, true freedom in the Spirit comes by the third night of revival when people realize I'm not here to be distant but to walk with them, to worship together.

Building trust is essential. I start with my testimony, sharing God's Word to plant seeds, creating rapport, so they know I'm a real person who has faced life's challenges. When leading a revival, that trust is vital. They need to know I'm guiding them to the throne of God in new dimensions and that I'll speak from the Word of God with compassion and humility. **Proverbs 3:5** reminds us, *"Trust in the LORD with all thine heart; and lean not unto thine own understanding."*

As I minister, I get to know each person in the Spirit. They are my children in the Lord, regardless of age, and I yearn to see their spiritual growth. It's a joy to watch them move in the gifts of the Spirit, to see the message of faith take root, and to watch them step into God's calling. **3 John 1:4** says, *"I have no greater joy than to hear that my children walk in truth."* Night after night, seeing them progress in their walk with God fills my heart.

The Lord often leads me in a specific direction during

Vicki Jamison Peterson: God's Anointed Vessel

these services, and while He may lead you differently in your ministry, I hope that sharing what He has shown me will inspire you as you walk your own journey with Him. **1 Peter 4:10** encourages us, *"As every man hath received the gift, even so minister the same one to another, as good stewards of the manifold grace of God."* May we each learn from the Spirit, growing in grace and truth as we lead others to worship in spirit and in truth.

"Faith in Action: Breaking Strongholds and Standing for Christ"

In ministry, you learn from the faithful examples of those like Kenneth Copeland, Fred Price, and John Sene—each dedicated to breaking strongholds through worship. I enter every congregation expecting revival, no matter how spiritually dry it may feel. **2 Corinthians 10:4** (KJV) reminds us, *"For the weapons of our warfare are not carnal, but mighty through God to the pulling down of strong holds."* Recently, I ministered in one of the most traditional, spiritually dormant churches I've encountered. Everything in me wanted to walk out, thinking, *Am I in the wrong place?* But God had a visitation planned for that congregation.

I began to let the love of God flow, reaching the people in kindness, and then I started singing in the Spirit. Slowly, they began to sing along, and as we persisted, the Spirit of God visited the congregation in a way they had never experienced before. **1 John 4:4** says, *"Ye

are of God, little children, and have overcome them: because greater is he that is in you, than he that is in the world."* When we trust in the power of Christ within us, we can break through even the hardest hearts.

It's essential not to speak negatively about those you minister to, no matter the spiritual state you find them in. Enter every situation confident in Christ, declaring, *"**I can do all things through Christ which strengtheneth me"*** **(Philippians 4:13 KJV).** This mindset allowed a revival to continue for two weeks in Salem, Ohio, with people's lives transformed night after night.

On another occasion, I received a surprising call. Years before, I had interviewed a woman on a television program called *It's a New Day*. She had shared her testimony, detailing a troubled past and a glorious redemption through Christ. Tragically, she and her husband passed away in a car accident. Her family's attorney contacted me, asking if I would serve as a key witness in the trial against the company responsible for the accident. They wanted me to testify about her transformed life, with the defense claiming her testimony on television was merely scripted entertainment.

The defense had accessed the interview tape, attempting to paint her testimony as a fabricated story to discredit her faith transformation. However, **2 Corinthians 5:17** (KJV) says, *"**Therefore if any man be in Christ, he is a new creature: old things are passed away; behold, all things are become new."*** The defense sought to highlight her past, ignoring the power of her rebirth in Christ.

Vicki Jamison Peterson: God's Anointed Vessel

Under pressure, especially with the media network facing scrutiny from the FCC, I was prepared to testify truthfully, even about technical aspects like editing. I was there to stand as a witness, not just for this woman's story, but for the testimony of Jesus Christ. **Romans 1:16** (KJV) says, *"For I am not ashamed of the gospel of Christ: for it is the power of God unto salvation to every one that believeth."* Standing for Christ, even in a courtroom, is an opportunity to let the power of God shine forth, reminding the world of His ability to transform lives completely.

Through each ministry experience, I've seen that God uses us to reach others, sometimes through challenges and always with His strength guiding us.

"Guided by the Spirit: The Power of Intercession and Divine Intervention"

I didn't understand all the legal terminology involved, but I was ready to go if God wanted me to. As the trial approached, toward the end of the Salem revival, it struck me that I could be called at any moment. I walked down to the dining room where Phil and Fern Halverson were sitting and mentioned my concern about the case. They just smiled knowingly, and I realized they had been interceding about this situation—praying for the insurance settlement, for the children's support, and for a resolution. **Romans 8:26** (KJV) tells us, *"Likewise the Spirit also helpeth our infirmities: for we know not what we should pray for as we ought: but the Spirit itself maketh intercession for us with groanings which cannot be uttered."*

Phil shared that he had specifically prayed that the little one, who was disabled and needed lifelong care, would be supported. Upon returning to Dallas, my mother informed me that the attorney's office had called—it looked like I would need to travel to the border that week. But in my spirit, I sensed I wouldn't need to go. The next day, no further word came, so we followed up, and they told us the case had started but had been settled out of court. The child was cared for, and I didn't have to take that trip. God had moved on our behalf through the intercession of the Holy Spirit. **Psalm 37:5** reminds us, *"Commit thy way unto the LORD; trust also in him; and he shall bring it to pass."*

This experience taught me the importance of yielding to the Spirit's intercession. If it is this vital in my life, isn't it just as crucial in yours and in the lives of those around you? The Holy Spirit never prays selfishly; He desires everyone's victory. **Romans 12:18** says, *"If it be possible, as much as lieth in you, live peaceably with all men."* The Spirit wants us all to come out winners.

I also saw this when Wes and I had to organize our ministry and personal lives legally. As we discussed our assets with the attorney, I realized that in each matter, the Spirit desired a fair outcome for all. **1 Corinthians 14:33** reminds us, *"For God is not the author of confusion, but of peace, as in all churches of the saints."* The Spirit led us to clarity, ensuring both our ministry and personal needs were understood and met.

In moments like these, God's guidance brings peace and order, showing that He truly works all things together for our good.

"The Spirit's Tapestry: God's Guidance in Ministry and Life"

As I worked with the attorney, I watched him go back and forth, weaving together our personal and ministry lives until everything was beautifully organized. Our lives, ministry, and finances were aligned, ensuring that both our board and the government would find everything in perfect order. **Proverbs 3:6** (KJV) says, *"In all thy ways acknowledge him, and he shall direct thy paths."* When I left, I told the attorney, "You showed me something today." He asked what I meant, and I replied, "You showed me the characteristic of the Holy Spirit that I needed to see."

I had often viewed things as black and white, but the Holy Spirit works patiently, understanding that while we may not always be completely right, others also have a voice. He is interested in bringing harmony even when we don't agree, interceding on behalf of everyone involved. **Romans 8:27** affirms, *"And he that searcheth the hearts knoweth what is the mind of the Spirit, because he maketh intercession for the saints according to the will of God."* The Spirit weaves a tapestry of our lives, creating a sweet fragrance to the

Father in every area.

In New Orleans, night after night, we saw people saved. After each service, we would go for coffee, and I sensed that we were supposed to take the message to the streets. While the Holy Spirit gave me the desire, I struggled with it. I thought, *I'm comfortable in air-conditioned rooms with familiar surroundings,* but deep within, there was a stirring—a little "rodeo." Some of you know what I mean. You may appear calm and polished, but inside, there's a spirit ready to leap into action. **Psalm 37:4** (KJV) encourages us, *"Delight thyself also in the LORD; and he shall give thee the desires of thine heart."*

The Holy Spirit often places desires in our hearts that challenge us, urging us into new areas of ministry. Though I was initially hesitant to minister on the streets, the Spirit was teaching me to step beyond my comfort zone, letting go of preferences for the sake of reaching souls. **Isaiah 55:8-9** reminds us, *"For my thoughts are not your thoughts, neither are your ways my ways, saith the LORD."* He has plans beyond our understanding, woven together in ways we can't fully see.

Through every step of this journey, God shows us that He cares about our lives down to the details, urging us forward with love and purpose.

** "Stepping Out in Faith: Bold

Vicki Jamison Peterson: God's Anointed Vessel

Ministry in Unexpected Places"**

Don't be fooled by appearances—God knows what's inside, and He won't ask you to do something you won't ultimately enjoy. Even if you hesitate at first, the Spirit guides with purpose. **Jeremiah 1:5** (KJV) reminds us, *"Before I formed thee in the belly I knew thee; and before thou camest forth out of the womb I sanctified thee, and I ordained thee a prophet unto the nations."* Night after night, I sensed God prompting me to go into the streets and reach the lost in the French Quarter, not just from an air-conditioned building, but out among the people.

There, people were carousing and indulging in sin. The Spirit urged me to leave the comfort of our building and take Jesus to the streets. After a particularly challenging service, I knew we had to shake things up. The people seemed stuck in place, so I called everyone to their feet, saying, *"The joy of the Lord is my strength!"* We marched around the building, stirring up praise. Like **Joshua 6:5**, where the walls of Jericho fell after a faithful march, our praise broke through spiritual barriers.

I challenged them, "How many are willing to go out into the streets for Jesus?" About 35 hands shot up. Not wasting time, we prayed over them, sealing their commitment before doubts could creep in. **Mark 16:15** says, *"Go ye into all the world, and preach the gospel to every creature."* The next day, reality hit me—I didn't have experience leading street ministry. But God had never coddled me or waited until I felt entirely ready. Instead, He simply says, *"Go,"* and I obey.

God doesn't always ease us in; sometimes He thrusts us forward. I felt like a child being lifted up and encouraged with visions of what could happen, and I'd get excited, even if part of me was nervous. Then God would push me into action, and I'd go, sometimes facing unexpected challenges. **2 Corinthians 12:9** assures us, *"My grace is sufficient for thee: for my strength is made perfect in weakness."* Even after rough experiences, I've found God's encouragement waiting, reminding me of the joy that came from stepping out in faith.

The Spirit nudges us to embrace boldness, and though there may be struggle or sacrifice, each step forward brings His purpose and peace.

"Empowered by Eternity: Embracing the Call with Courage"**

"Lord, I'm a lady," I protested, but He would point to a soul on the brink of eternity, ready to draw me into action again. The Spirit would prompt me, often with a little nudge, a reminder that His eternal mission was greater than my comfort or fears. Sometimes I'd feel hesitant, like being pulled along, yet something in me loved the adventure. **Jeremiah 1:7** (KJV) says, *"But the LORD said unto me, Say not, I am a child: for thou shalt go to all that I shall send thee, and whatsoever I command thee thou shalt speak."*

Vicki Jamison Peterson: God's Anointed Vessel

When the Spirit imparts eternity, this world fades in comparison. He gives strength to go forward, even alone if necessary. **Matthew 28:20** reminds us, *"And, lo, I am with you always, even unto the end of the world."* Knowing that we walk with God allows us to press on, regardless of the obstacles. My prayer today is that each of you would receive an impartation of eternity in your hearts, igniting an unquenchable passion for souls.

Preparing for our outreach to the French Quarter, I realized I had little experience in street ministry. As we gathered, we prayed and worshiped, sensing God's presence and purpose. I instructed everyone to walk in silence, three or four abreast, down the sidewalk. "We are the army of the Lord," I told them, and when I gave the signal, they began singing. **Psalm 100:1-2** reminds us, *"Make a joyful noise unto the LORD, all ye lands. Serve the LORD with gladness: come before his presence with singing."*

With powerful voices singing, *"The joy of the Lord is my strength,"* we filled the streets with praises that drew attention and softened hearts. As we sang, God's Spirit moved through the crowd, drawing people closer. Just as **Isaiah 55:12** (KJV) proclaims, *"For ye shall go out with joy, and be led forth with peace,"* our joy overflowed, inviting others to witness the peace and strength found in Christ.

This experience taught me that when God calls, He equips. Whether it's in comfort or out in the unknown,

His Spirit empowers us to walk in faith, to sing with courage, and to share the eternal hope we carry.

As we walked down Bourbon Street on a Saturday night, where elegance and revelry mingled with sin, the Spirit led us to stop under an ornate balcony. People dressed in their finest dined and drank above us. And then, I heard His voice say, "Stop here and speak." Unsure of how to start, I began with what I knew: *"For many years, I have been a housewife."* It drew laughs, but it was a start. Then, I sang "Amazing Grace," filling the air with words of hope. **Psalm 96:1** (KJV) reminds us, *"O sing unto the LORD a new song: sing unto the LORD, all the earth."*

After I shared, I handed the mic to one of our young men, who boldly announced, *"You're all going to hell!"* Startled, I took the mic back, gently correcting him, "We're here to tell them that all heaven's breaking loose, and the joy of the Lord is their strength." God's message was of love and salvation, not condemnation. **John 3:17** (KJV) tells us, *"For God sent not his Son into the world to condemn the world; but that the world through him might be saved."*

Then another young man took the mic, repeating, *"You're all going to hell."* I again redirected, emphasizing God's love, the true message of our mission. As we continued, the police arrived, alerted by hotel management that we were "disturbing the peace." But God's hand was with us. The officers, after

Vicki Jamison Peterson: God's Anointed Vessel

assessing, allowed us to continue. **Psalm 34:7** promises, *"The angel of the LORD encampeth round about them that fear him, and delivereth them."*

With renewed boldness, we filled the streets with joyful song, *"The joy of the Lord is my strength."* Singing, dancing, and jumping for joy, our message brought light into a place filled with darkness. *"If you want joy, you must sing for it... shout for it... jump for it!"* The joy we displayed became a witness to everyone watching. As we obeyed, the Lord turned even the simplest expressions of faith into profound moments of love and hope.

"The Joy of the Lord: Street Ministry, Spiritual Warfare, and Laughter in the Spirit"

We took to the streets singing with a joyful boldness, filling the New Orleans air with *"The joy of the Lord is my strength!"* As we walked, something amazing happened: people joined in, even those who hadn't planned to encounter God that night. Passing by a restaurant, we saw Japanese businessmen waiting in line for a show- yet there they were, singing along. God's Spirit was drawing people unexpectedly. *"Make a joyful noise unto the Lord, all ye lands. Serve the Lord with gladness"* (Psalm 100:1-2, KJV).

On that trip, Fern and Phil Halverson had sensed the Spirit calling them to pray for "Cajuns." Unsure of the meaning, they trusted God. Later, on the same New Orleans streets, they met a couple from Canada who were ready to accept Christ, realizing the Spirit had been guiding them all along. When they prayed with this couple, God's Word took root. The guidance of the Holy Spirit shows that He prepares hearts and guides each encounter. *"For as many as are led by the Spirit of God, they are the sons of God"* (Romans 8:14, KJV).

At one point, a young man selling flowers began to shout angrily at us, insisting we leave. Instead of arguing, I simply kept singing, *"The joy of the Lord is my strength."* And just like that, his anger melted away as he slipped into the night. Brother Kenneth Hagin's advice rang true that night: laugh at the devil! Just as he taught me, I had faith that laughter and joy would confound the enemy, for *"a merry heart doeth good like a medicine"* (Proverbs 17:22, KJV). And so we kept singing, praising God, letting His joy flow like a river into the lives we touched.

"Interceding in the Spirit: Lessons of Gratitude, Guidance, and Standing with God's Servants"

A few words come to mind when I think of Brother Hagin: kindness, wisdom, and a heart willing to nurture others in their walk with the Lord. Years ago, as I was stepping into the ministry of intercession, I struggled to understand how the Spirit could lead me to pray over things I didn't intellectually understand. It was Brother Hagin who brought clarity. One day, as we rode in his car, I confided in him, sharing that sometimes I would see things in prayer, like a "cookie" or "candy," and I had no idea what it meant. He simply laughed, then revealed to me, "That's what we call our grandchildren!" *"But

Vicki Jamison Peterson: God's Anointed Vessel

the Comforter, which is the Holy Ghost, whom the Father will send in my name, he shall teach you all things"* (John 14:26, KJV).

He lovingly explained how God speaks through the Spirit, guiding even when the mind does not understand. Brother Hagin's ministry continues to be a special blessing. The Word he taught was alive, sharper than any two-edged sword, and he has helped many to discern the Spirit's voice and purpose in their lives. This Bible school, this ministry, has taught us to understand the Word in our spirits, letting it become alive within us. I am ever grateful for his influence, knowing that without his guidance, I would not have survived spiritually. *"The steps of a good man are ordered by the Lord: and he delighteth in his way"* (Psalm 37:23, KJV).

Each day, I lift up Brother Hagin and his family in prayer, asking God to bless them spiritually, physically, and financially. Let us, too, uphold those in ministry, knowing that their work often faces unseen challenges. As Paul wrote, *"Pray without ceasing"* (1 Thessalonians 5:17, KJV). May we be ever grateful for those who help guide us and may we always lift them in prayer, letting the Spirit direct us in all things.

DR MICAEL H YEAGER
AUTHORS SUPERNATURAL EXPERIENCE

Engulfed in a Gasoline Tar fire.

I have experience on numerous occasions when God has divinely intervened. I can think of at least sixty times. Here are just ten times this has happened to me.

#1 when a gang leader was trying to kill me by stabbing me to death while coming out of Chicago in his car.

#2 While saving a young man's life from a motorcycle accident.

#3 A large mule deer was going to slam into me on my motorcycle while I was headed through Canada.

#4 My wife and I rolling down a cliff in our car. My newborn son Michael was up in the air, as my wife reaches out and snatches him to her chest.

#5 My seventh-month pregnant wife, my son Michael and I were on a 450 custom Honda. Headed for guardrails, telephone pole, and a pile of rocks.

#6 Supernaturally empowered while driving a motorcycle through communist infested lands.

#7 While flying my airplane through a set of high lines.

#8 Right before I slammed my Cadillac into a concrete bridge.

#9 Preventing a young lady from burning to death when her hair caught on fire.

#10 When I was engulfed in a Raging fire.

Everything around me exploded into fire! (Tears are filling my eyes as I share this incredible story of God's protection in the midst of my stupidity.) It all began as I

Vicki Jamison Peterson: God's Anointed Vessel

was stirring gasoline into a five-gallon bucket of black tar, thinning it to be spread on our Churches Steal roof! We had a thirty-gallon galvanized garbage can with an LP torch under this container melting the tar! The fumes ignited, and this massive wave of fire came rushing from about 20 feet away wholly engulfing me.

I mean I am entirely swallowed up in this gasoline and black tar fire. The two buckets of gasoline are burning at my feet. The bucket of tar and gasoline I was stirring is on fire. I had been using an excessive amount of gas to keep my hands, arms, and face free from tar. Gasoline is the only thing that would clean the black tar off me. My clothes are completely saturated in gasoline, as well as my hands, arms and face. I'm standing there in the midst of all of this fire with no FEAR in my heart. At the same Time my mind is quickened, but Time seems to have come to a standstill! I have complete and utter peace, but still knowing that I was in big trouble.

Back in 1980, I began to memorize and meditate on Scriptures declaring that fire could not consume me.

Isaiah 43:2, "When thou passest through the waters, I will be with thee; and through the rivers, they shall not overflow thee: when thou walkest through the fire, thou shalt not be burned ; neither shall the flame kindle upon thee."

I meditated on the scriptures because I kept burning myself with our woodstove. Through the years, I have maintained these scriptures in my heart. In the summer of 2014, I had an amazing experience when God used these scriptures to come to my rescue, otherwise, I would have been burned to death.

I can honestly tell you that I did not feel the heat, flames, or the fire upon me. I grabbed a metal canister and put it over the top of the one bucket of burning gas. I quickly found another canister that I could put over the other bucket. During this Time, I'm running in and out of the fire.

I'm not thinking; I'm just moving knowing that our gymnasium and our whole church could go up in flames at any moment. We are right up against the gymnasium with a house trailer right there. The apartment and the stairs to the apartment above our gymnasium were right there. I had to get the fire out, and I mean fast! Everything was on fire, including the ground where we had spilled tar and gas.

The whole place is nothing but an infernal. During this Time, Jesse had made his way around the flames nurturing his burnt arm, which he had received standing outside of the flames! He was trying to find a water hose we had lying there to water a small garden. I'm still running in and out of the flames, trying to put out this raging fire. Jesse had been through a terrible fire in the past, being seriously hurt. I could see that he was in the midst of some shock from the fire and the heat.

Right before my very eyes, the bucket that was filled with tar and gasoline had melted at my feet to less than 8 inches high. Now the flames were getting worse, they were reaching high into the sky. The men who have been spreading the mixture of tar and Gasoline come running seeing the flames on top of our Church Sanctuary. The

Vicki Jamison Peterson: God's Anointed Vessel

whole thing was nothing but a massive blaze. During this Time, brother Mark, who lives in the apartment up above, comes running out onto his apartment's deck. He sees everything that is happening.

Brother Jesse is wrestling with the water hose, trying to disconnect it from another hose to use it to fight the fire. I ran over and began to help him. And then I took the hoses from him, heading back into the fire. Praise God the water did the job even with gasoline and burning tar everywhere. We were able to douse the flames. Praise God, praise God, praise God the fire was out.

Things happened so fast at the Time that I did not even realize exactly the events that had transpired. But God in His grace and in His mercy once again protected me from my own massive stupidity. Jesse did receive burns on his right forearm. Amazingly, I did not receive one burn, not one singed hair, or even the smell of smoke on me. All of the gas that was on me, my hands, my face, and my clothes never ignited. God is so good! His Mercy Endures Forever!

CHAPTER SIX

"Heaven on Bourbon Street: Obedience, Intercession, and the Power of Praise"

As we gathered to pray, my heart was stirred with a sense of urgency to lift up those in need. I felt the call to intercede on their behalf and to bless them for all they've done. With faith and boldness, we began our intercession, seeking the Lord's favor and protection over their lives. The Spirit led me to rejoice, and I couldn't help but laugh—a laugh of freedom and joy in the Lord. *"**The joy of the LORD is your strength**"* **(Nehemiah 8:10, KJV).** It was as if that joy melted away any barrier, causing opposition to fade like snow under the summer sun.

Moving on, we walked down the dim streets, reaching a spot where the Lord commanded, "Stop here." I halted, hearing His instruction clearly: "Lift your hands and sing." The street was alive with elegance—fine restaurants, well-dressed patrons. Yet, I closed my eyes to silence every distraction, determined to obey. Sometimes, following the Spirit means letting go of self-

Vicki Jamison Peterson: God's Anointed Vessel

consciousness, surrendering fully to God. As I lifted my hands, I began to sing:

"Then sings my soul, my Savior God, to Thee, How great Thou art! How great Thou art!"

The song filled the air, and as I praised, people were drawn out of the buildings and restaurants. One by one, they stopped, listening, and soon joined in worship on the sidewalks of Bourbon Street. Heaven had visited that dark corner, and the presence of God was so tangible, it felt as if His cloud of glory covered us. For those moments, I didn't care who saw or what they thought—I was lost in worship, consumed with a love for Jesus. The power of praise unlocked doors that night. People were saved; one young man even tossed away a hundred dollars' worth of drugs, receiving Jesus right there. From then on, he carried our PA system, lifting it high like a banner of hope over the streets.

The lost—those searching for meaning in all the wrong places—encountered the very presence of an all-knowing, ever-loving Father. They heard songs that perhaps their mothers and grandparents once sang to them, songs that echoed in their hearts, sparking memories of innocence and hope. While they had come to Bourbon Street seeking pleasure, they found something far greater: the overwhelming love of Jesus. ***"For the Son of man is come to seek and to save that which was lost"* (Luke 19:10, KJV).**

We'll never know the full impact of that night, but I'm certain it was the intercessory prayers beforehand that opened the doors. It was prayer that released the angels of God to protect and direct us, even when we unknowingly operated without the needed permit for the loudspeaker. God knew He wanted a voice of praise on Bourbon Street, and He ensured we had the freedom to share it. The Lord desires for His light to reach every corner, whether the refined establishments or the street corners filled with people searching for fulfillment.

I believe that some of you will feel that same call, that you'll be led by the Spirit to go into places where His light needs to shine. *"**Go out into the highways and hedges, and compel them to come in, that my house may be filled**"* **(Luke 14:23, KJV).** I challenge you to be His vessel, to go forth with courage, and to let God's love and power flow through you, even in the places least expected.

"Leave No Stone Unturned: Walking in the Full Armor of God"

I have a message that's close to my heart, and I want to share it with you straight from the Word of God. I've been in ministry for many years, and although that's not as long as others, it's been long enough for God to reveal His truth and power in ways I never imagined. I may not always be as fiery or outspoken, but the fire of God is consuming me tonight because I've been brought back from the brink of destruction, and I'm here to testify: God is a deliverer!

Vicki Jamison Peterson: God's Anointed Vessel

I want to talk to you about leaving no stone unturned. Say it with me, "Leave no stone unturned." I'll share what I've learned about walking in strength and victory by fully embracing God's Word and His armor. Let's start in Ephesians 6. In verses 10 and 11, the Apostle Paul says, *"**Finally, my brethren, be strong in the Lord, and in the power of his might. Put on the whole armour of God, that ye may be able to stand against the wiles of the devil**"* **(Ephesians 6:10-11, KJV).** This is where we learn to "leave no stone unturned," putting on every piece of armor God has given.

You see, one of the greatest blessings I received was having a spiritual father like Kenneth Hagan, who taught me to rely on God's Word above everything else. Even with the gifts of the Spirit in operation, he would remind us that without the Word as our foundation, we might miss the highest and best. Signs, wonders, and miracles are amazing, and I love witnessing them. But when I walk into a service, I'm always armed with the Word first. **Hebrews 4:12** reminds us, *"**For the word of God is quick, and powerful, and sharper than any twoedged sword…**"* **(KJV).** The Word is what delivers and sets us free.

When I look back over my life and see all that I've faced, I know God did not create me—or you—to fail. He created us for success in Him. He has a purpose for each of us, and part of that purpose is to live in victory. But that requires commitment and action on our part. We are to leave no stone unturned in our pursuit of God's armor and truth. **Ephesians 6:13** tells us, *"**Wherefore take unto you the whole armour of God, that ye may be** able to withstand in the evil day, and having done all, to stand"* (KJV).**

Friends, let's decide not to leave anything behind. Commit to living each day clothed in His armor, equipped with His Word, and empowered by His Spirit. As we do, we'll be able to stand strong and walk in the victory He has prepared for us.

"Equipped for Battle: Embracing the Full Armor of God"

In our lives as believers, we are in a constant battle, but it's not against flesh and blood or mere human opposition. As Paul reminds us in Ephesians, *"**For we wrestle not against flesh and blood, but against principalities, against powers, against the rulers of the darkness of this world, against spiritual wickedness in high places"*** (Ephesians 6:12, KJV). Our battle is with the unseen forces of darkness, and for that, we must be fully prepared. God has provided us with all we need, giving us His armor to stand firm and prevail.

So, let us put on this **"armor of God"** so that we may withstand the enemy on the day of evil. *"**Stand therefore, having your loins girt about with truth, and having on the breastplate of righteousness; And your feet shod with the preparation of the gospel of peace; Above all, taking the shield of faith, wherewith ye shall be able to quench all the fiery darts of the wicked. And take the helmet of salvation, and the**

Vicki Jamison Peterson: God's Anointed Vessel

sword of the Spirit, which is the word of God"* (Ephesians 6:14-17, KJV).

God equips us with the tools for victory: His Son for our salvation, His Spirit to comfort and strengthen us, and His Word to guide us. But we must take this armor and actively use it in our lives, knowing that God is not limited to one way of working. Often, it is in the most desperate times that we are willing to surrender fully and do whatever it takes to be healed, set free, or receive answers.

Some time ago, the Lord gave me a promise: *"You'll be married soon."* At the time, I wasn't even thinking about marriage and had no candidates in sight. But when God speaks, He brings His words to pass in ways beyond our understanding. Shortly afterward, I met Dr. Carl R. Peterson, a Spirit-filled psychiatrist, who was everything God had promised and more. We quickly realized that not only had God brought us together in marriage, but He also planned for us to merge prayer with medicine. Dr. Peterson was given a unique gift to combine wisdom, revelation, and the latest medical knowledge. Now, through his practice, he prays over patients, often seeing the miraculous unfold as people rise from wheelchairs and are restored in both body and mind.

This is God's wisdom at work, empowering us for His calling. Let us take up our armor, walk in His strength, and trust in His boundless ability to work in ways that surpass human limits.

"Faith in Action: Leaving No Stone Unturned in the Journey to Healing"

Throughout my years of ministry, I witnessed people with "incurable" conditions be restored by the power of God, healed mentally, spiritually, and physically. God often works in unexpected ways, sometimes giving divine revelation to those in the medical field who are devoted to Him. One such person was my husband, who had a unique gift for combining prayer with his medical expertise. Little did I know that he would later play a critical role in my journey to healing.

Years of constant ministry, traveling, and preaching wore my body down. Week after week, I poured out my energy, sometimes preaching into the night and rising at dawn to catch another plane to the next city. Eventually, my physical strength was depleted, and in November of that year, I was struck with a severe, traumatic illness that caused rapid deterioration. Each day, I felt weaker, but I refused to give up. I knew the importance of faith in action; though I felt unwell, I would get up, wash my hair, and dress myself each morning, believing that my healing was coming.

The Bible says in **James 2:17 (KJV), *"Even so faith, if it hath not works, is dead, being alone."*** True faith compels action. We cannot sit idly, waiting for healing to descend without moving in faith toward it. Though miraculous healings do occur, God often calls us to pursue healing actively. So, despite my weakness, I continued to press on, determined not to remain stagnant

Vicki Jamison Peterson: God's Anointed Vessel

in my illness.

At one point, a doctor performed a test that showed a possible blood clot or tumor in my brainstem. The news was grim—if this was the case, there would be no medical solution. This is the kind of news that shakes you to your core. But my faith reminded me of the words in **Psalm 46:1 (KJV), *"God is our refuge and strength, a very present help in trouble."***

I was later assigned a new doctor, Pat Lindsay, who took a unique approach to my case. She took my blood pressure, then asked me to stand, taking it again. *"Bingo,"* she said. *"Just what I thought."* She explained that my blood pressure wasn't rising upon standing, causing my brain to lack the blood supply it needed. This revelation was key, and I knew this was God's provision. For me, seeking medical care was part of leaving no stone unturned. As Jesus said, *"**They that are whole need not a physician; but they that are sick**"* **(Luke 5:31, KJV)**. God places knowledgeable, compassionate people like Dr. Lindsay in our lives to aid in our healing.

When you're battling illness, you are willing to do whatever it takes to get well, even if that means seeking help from others. Dr. Lindsay was not only a skilled physician but a person of prayer. She committed to an hour of intercessory prayer for me daily, asking her nurse to do the same, because, as she told me, *"The medicine alone can't do it. Your condition is so severe that only intercessory prayer will make it work."*

Thank God for people of faith and prayer who stand with us! Through their prayers and my own faith-driven actions, God continued to work in my body, bringing me through this time of trial.

Jesus said, *"**They that are whole have no need of the physician, but they that are sick**"* (Mark 2:17, KJV). As a faith minister and married to a doctor, I've come to understand the balance between divine healing and medical support. I've witnessed my husband—a physician with a compassionate heart and a prayerful spirit—serve patients with both his medical expertise and a genuine love for their healing. In my journey, I've learned that God works through various avenues, and He certainly uses medical professionals to carry out His work.

My husband, like other doctors dedicated to God, doesn't see patients as statistics. He doesn't lose sleep because he doubts his skills but because he cares deeply. Many times, when he's lacked the answers, the Holy Spirit has given him guidance beyond the reach of ordinary knowledge. Not all doctors may understand spiritual gifts, but it's clear that God's hand can work through them, revealing solutions for those willing to seek His wisdom.

For those in desperate need, this can be a lifeline. When my own health deteriorated, I sought every possible way to be restored. *"**The effectual fervent prayer of a righteous man availeth much**"* (James 5:16, KJV), and I was grateful for prayer warriors, like my husband and others, who interceded for me. At one point, my

Vicki Jamison Peterson: God's Anointed Vessel

doctor, who understood both medical science and the power of prayer, took my case to heart. She told me that in my state, only intercessory prayer would activate the healing alongside the medicine. She promised an hour of prayer each day and even asked her nurse to pray with her in the Spirit for my healing. How blessed we are to have people who stand in prayer for us!

During this time, I experienced the reality of **Psalm 91:15 (KJV),** where God says, *"**I will be with him in trouble; I will deliver him, and honour him.**"* I realized I had to leave no stone unturned. When my legs became so weak that I could barely walk and my speech faltered, I would still get up, dress, and go out with friends, even though talking was hard. My husband would take me to the shopping center, supporting me as I walked, making sure my muscles didn't deteriorate further. I felt imprisoned in my own body, but I refused to stay down. In faith, I acted as though I were whole, trusting God to bring me through.

Sometimes, people of faith can misunderstand illness, choosing to deny it rather than stand with the one suffering. But facing the reality of illness doesn't undermine faith; it strengthens it. Even if healing comes through a "gift horse" sent by God, I won't look it in the mouth—I'll praise God for the answer He sends.

Through these challenging times, I've learned that healing often requires a partnership of prayer, medicine, and unwavering faith. Leaving no stone unturned means doing all we can while waiting on God's power to bring us through.

"Faith in Action: The Power of Prayer, Persistence, and Community"

In my journey through sickness, I've seen that illness isn't something anyone plans. But even through the darkest days, faith always lights the way. During a particularly challenging season, my husband Carl took care of me with such kindness, making sure I was comfortable and happy. He'd make me milkshakes each night, helping me keep my strength. Though my situation was serious, I held on to joy and to the love of those around me. Carl would say, "If you ever become a little old lady, you'll be a sweet one," which was his way of lifting my spirits. I wasn't prepared for the illness, but it taught me to appreciate every bit of care and compassion, from Carl's attentiveness to the prayers of others.

I didn't know the battle I was about to face, but God had already moved others to intercede. In Santa Maria, as I stood to minister at my first speaking engagement after the illness, I learned that a month earlier, a preacher had paused mid-sermon and urged the congregation to intercede for me. Even before my symptoms appeared, the Holy Spirit was at work, preparing a network of prayers. *"**The effectual fervent prayer of a righteous man availeth much**"* **(James 5:16, KJV).** If God puts someone on your heart, don't ignore it! Pray for them. You might be the vital link they need.

Recovery wasn't smooth or quick. One evening, Carl

Vicki Jamison Peterson: God's Anointed Vessel

suggested a fast-paced walk around the neighborhood to help me regain strength. I clung to his arm, trusting that my strength would return. Suddenly, I felt my body give way, and I stumbled, nearly falling into the street. Carl caught me just in time, but to onlookers, it must have looked like I was severely ill. When we returned home, Carl checked my muscles, trying to find the root of the problem, yet even he was puzzled.

Despite these setbacks, my faith remained. I woke each morning believing that today would be the day I'd feel normal again—that I could walk, think, and live without limitations. It's amazing what we take for granted until we're unable to do it. So many who are disabled or recovering from strokes understand this. They may struggle to communicate, but they understand, they feel, and they want to connect. We should never ignore or avoid them out of discomfort. Rather, we should approach them with love, kindness, and respect, knowing they are valued by God and fully present.

Through it all, I learned the power of community in the body of Christ. Each person's prayers, each small act of kindness, helped me press on. With God's guidance and strength, I'll keep moving forward, and I encourage everyone to embrace their part in His body, lifting each other up in faith and love.

As believers, we're called to look beyond appearances, to see with hearts of compassion and hope. When you see someone in a wheelchair or with a visible struggle, it's not a time to look away. Instead, offer a smile, engage — show them that they are seen and valued. I've been in that place of struggle. I've faced moments that left me feeling like I'd lost everything, even hope. One morning, on Christmas Eve, I reached my lowest point. I confided to my husband, Carl, "I've lost hope." He saw my struggle and went straight to God, pleading for a breakthrough for his wife.

That day, Carl felt God had given him a revelation—a chemical deficiency in my brain was causing my symptoms. He said, "Doctors don't treat family, but I'll pray, and you'll have to seek the Lord on this." With faith, I took the medication, trusting that this was the answer God had provided. Within hours, I experienced a change—I could walk without wavering, without needing walls to hold me up. And though the medication wasn't a complete cure, it gave me a glimpse of recovery and hope.

Psalm 103:3 says, *"Who forgiveth all thine iniquities; who healeth all thy diseases"* (KJV). This promise anchored me as I walked each day in faith, even when the symptoms persisted. God's provision was in motion, even when my body struggled.

Yet, the road to full restoration was still winding. The illness was so consuming that at times it seemed my only options were a mental institution or a nursing home. This wasn't just a physical battle; it attacked my spirit and mind. I felt isolated and overwhelmed, often unable to make simple decisions, like choosing between parakeet seed and bird seed. Even in those moments, I clung to faith and continued acting as if I was healed. I went to the grocery store, prayed, and held on, trusting that God was

Vicki Jamison Peterson: God's Anointed Vessel

sustaining me.

Each day, I took small steps, standing on God's word. Even when it seemed I had little strength, I believed God was my source of healing and strength. *"**The Lord is my light and my salvation; whom shall I fear? The Lord is the strength of my life; of whom shall I be afraid?"** (Psalm 27:1, KJV).* And each day, I moved forward with this verse in my heart, trusting that God was carrying me through every uncertain step.

"Leaving No Stone Unturned: A Journey Through Healing, Faith, and Miracles"

I know what it feels like to be on the verge of losing everything—even my very self. At one point, my body was close to failing completely, and I understood the reality of becoming a mere shell of who I once was. I've been down the roads of sickness and frailty, to the point of being a cripple. Yet through it all, I learned that God doesn't overlook anything—He leaves no stone unturned.

A dear friend, Rex Broberg, came back to Tulsa to help in the office around the beginning of January. When he arrived, he said, "I'm bringing strength," and at that moment, I knew that God was sending me people to lift me up. Then, one Sunday evening, a friend called unexpectedly and told us to turn on PTL (Praise the Lord) Network. There, on the screen, an old recording of me from six months prior was playing. I sat and watched as my own voice declared boldly, "You are being healed! Your brain chemicals are being healed in the name of Jesus!" God had orchestrated this moment, reminding me that He knew my every need.

*"**And my God shall supply all your need according to his riches in glory by Christ Jesus**"* **(Philippians 4:19, KJV).** This scripture echoed in my heart as I realized that God's provision extended beyond the physical—He was healing my mind and spirit as well.

Only God could be so intricate and deliberate. At times, I feel like shouting and dancing because this journey has been overwhelming yet miraculous. I've walked every difficult road, faced every dark valley, and that's why I'm here, seeking to share hope and healing with you. I don't come here to simply talk; I come because I believe in the miraculous. I believe in it because I am one.

You see, we can't be passive in faith. My husband, as a psychiatrist, often talks about "passive-aggressive" personalities—those who subtly manipulate while appearing sweet and composed. But in this journey of faith, there's no room for passivity. *"**For the kingdom of God suffereth violence, and the violent take it by force**"* **(Matthew 11:12, KJV).** True faith is bold and unwavering.

When it comes to matters of the spirit, I stand firm. I call things as I see them—or rather, as I believe them. Through faith, God has called us to rise, to move forward without doubt or fear, and to claim the promises He has

Vicki Jamison Peterson: God's Anointed Vessel

given us. That's why I'm here, expecting miracles for each of you, because I know the power of God firsthand. And I know He wants to work that power in your life, too.

I was scheduled to leave on January 12th for California to preach. Despite my struggles, we didn't cancel a single engagement. That Thursday, at seven in the morning, I boarded the plane, though I felt weak and unsteady. A man sat next to me who knew who I was, and as we talked, I must've sounded like a yo-yo, trying to maintain conversation when I could barely manage a coherent thought. When we landed in Dallas, they had a cart waiting to take me to my next gate because walking was difficult, and my words were still shaky.

Once in Los Angeles, they met me with a wheelchair, and as I was being wheeled through the airport, three ladies came up and asked, "Are you Vicki Jamison?" I thought for a moment how I wished I'd said, "No, never heard of her!" But instead, I said, "Yes." Their faces dropped, and they asked, "Oh honey, what's wrong?" I smiled and said, "Oh, I'm going to be okay." I couldn't bring myself to tell them that I was on my way to a healing service to preach and pray for others when I could barely sit up. But despite my condition, my faith was fully intact. God was with me.

"But my God shall supply all your need according to his riches in glory by Christ Jesus" **(Philippians 4:19, KJV)**. I have relied on this promise through thick and thin. I learned long ago to put faith into action. So, even though I was being wheeled through that airport, I was not letting go of my belief that healing was mine.

There are times when we sit around waiting for a miracle when God has already provided the tools to start the journey. If He has provided a medicine, a doctor, or another means, why should I sit idle? Faith demands action. *"**For as the body without the spirit is dead, so faith without works is dead also**"* **(James 2:26, KJV).** I've learned that faith is a partnership with God; it's not about waiting idly but walking forward with the means He's placed before us.

Once, when my budget wasn't met and I had no way to get home, I took out my Bible, turned to Philippians 4:19, and held it up to God, reading it out loud. I said, "God, if my needs aren't met, I'll tell everyone. But if it's true, I'll lay my life down for it." And in that moment, God came through. That's how I know, beyond all doubt, that God is my source. We don't have to cling to a cliff and ignore His provision like the man who prayed for help only to turn away the helicopter God had sent.

Faith is moving forward, trusting that God has made the way and will supply every need. He has been faithful to meet my needs, and He will be faithful to meet yours. If He has provided the means, then don't wait—take the step. Let's leave no stone unturned in our walk with Him.

DR MICAEL H YEAGER
AUTHORS SUPERNATURAL EXPERIENCE

THEY COULD NOT MOVE or SPEAK for 2 1/2 HOURS

My family and I travelled out West ministering in different churches and visiting relatives in Wisconsin. We were invited to speak at a church in Minneapolis, Minnesota. The pastor had two different churches that he pastored. One of these churches was in the suburbs, and the other one was in the heart of Minneapolis. The larger of the two churches was in the suburbs.

I was to minister at the larger church first and then immediately go to his other church downtown. The whole congregation was in the same service that morning. There were approximately 140 to 160 people including women, men, children, and babies in the sanctuary.

As I began to speak, I found myself unexpectedly speaking on the subject of The year that King Uzia died, I saw the Lord high and lifted up, and his glory filled the Temple, which is found in the book of Isaiah! The unction of the Holy Ghost was upon me so strong that it just flowed out of my belly like rivers of living water. To this day I do not remember everything that I said. As I was speaking, I sensed an amazing heavenly touch of God's presence on myself and everyone in the sanctuary.

The spirit of God was on me in a mighty way, and yet I was aware of the time factor. To get to Pastor Bill's sister church downtown Minnesota, I was not going to have time to lay hands on or pray for any-one. If God were going to confirm his word with signs following, then he would have to do it without me being there.

It turns out that is exactly what God wanted to do! When I was at the limit of the amount of the time allotted to me, I quickly closed with a prayer. I did not say anything to the pastor or anyone else as I grabbed my Bible to leave the sanctuary. My family was already loaded up and waiting for me in our vehicle. As I ran out the door, I perceived something strange, awesome and wonderful was beginning to happen to the congregation. There was a heavy, amazing and holy hush that had come upon them.

By the time I arrived at the other church, their worship had already begun. As I stood up in the pulpit to Minister God's Word, the Holy Spirit began to speak to me again, with a completely, totally different message. God did wonderful things in the sister church downtown that afternoon as I preached a message on being radically sold out and committed to Christ.

Everyone ended up falling out of their chairs to the floor on their faces, weeping and crying before the Lord. This is not something I have ever encouraged any congregation to do. I have seen this happen numerous times where I simply have to stop preaching because the presence of God is so strong, and so real that people cannot stay in their seats. I would stop preaching, get on my face, and just wait on God, as he moved on the people's hearts.

After that service, we went back to our fifth wheel trailer

Vicki Jamison Peterson: God's Anointed Vessel

at the local campgrounds where we were camping. Later in the day, I received a phone call from this pastor. He was acting rather strangely and speaking very softly in a very hushed manner.

He asked me with a whisper: does that always happen after you are done preaching? I said to him, tell me what happened. He said, "As you were headed out the door, I began to melt to the floor, I could not keep standing, and I found myself pinned to the floor of the sanctuary. I could not move or speak." Now all the children (including babies) were in the sanctuary with the rest of the congregation. He said he could not move for two and a half hours. During this whole experience, he did not hear another sound in the facility. For over two and a half hours he just simply laid there not being able to move or speak a word under the presence and mighty hand of God. After two and a half hours Pastor Bill was able to move finally, and to get up.

He had thought for sure that he was the only one still left in the church. Everybody must have gone home a long time ago, and that he was there by himself. But to his complete shock and amazement, everybody was still there, lying on the floor. Nobody could move or speak for over two and a half hours! Men, women, children and even the babies were still lying on the floor, not moving, talking, or crying! God was in the house! The tangible, overwhelming, solemn, presence and holiness of God had come!

Pastor Bill asked me to come over to his house so we could talk about what happened that day in his church service. My family and I arrived. He invited us inside. He asked if this normally happens wherever I went. I informed him, no, but many wonderful and strange things do take place. It did not always happen, except when I get myself in a place of complete, absolute surrender and submission to Jesus Christ. This submission included not putting ANYTHING else but the WORD of God into my heart. When I simply seek the face of God, by praying, giving myself completely to the word, meditation, singing and worship, intimacy with the Father, Son, and Holy Ghost, this was the result! God is not a respecter of people, what he does for one, he will do for others!

CHAPTER SEVEN

"Hold On to Faith: Embracing God's Help in Unseen Ways"

The story of the man stranded on a cliff praying for God's help captures our struggle perfectly. As he clung to that branch, God sent him not one, but three helicopters. Each time, he refused the help, insisting he was waiting on God alone. When he finally reached heaven, he asked St. Peter, "Why did I die? I was believing God!" St. Peter answered, "I sent a helicopter three times for you." We often have our minds made up about how God *should* help us, insisting on our way, but we must learn to remain open to whatever form His help takes. Sometimes, God sends a lifeline we'd never expect—a doctor, a friend, or a timely word on a billboard.

"Except ye be converted, and become as little children, ye shall not enter into the kingdom of heaven" (Matthew 18:3, KJV). God wants us to approach Him with the humility and openness of a child, ready to receive whatever He offers, however He chooses

to work.

One night, I arrived at a service feeling incredibly weak, dragging a luggage rack, dizzy and barely able to comb my hair. I stood there, leading worship, and the only song I could remember was "Blessed Assurance, Jesus is mine." We sang it together, then moved into a simple "Hallelujah" chorus that even I couldn't forget. As I kept singing, people began to be healed, and I felt strength returning to my body. God was moving through the simplicity of our faith, meeting us in that moment, and by the end, I could feel myself walking more steadily.

The next morning, though, I felt like I could barely make it out of bed, my soul echoing words I didn't want to believe: "You're dying." But I knew better than to let the enemy's lies control my heart. God had called me to preach, not to give in to fear. *"**Fight the good fight of faith, lay hold on eternal life**"* **(1 Timothy 6:12, KJV).** I was determined to fight this fight, standing in the power of God's promises. That Sunday morning, as I preached, people in the congregation were healed all around the auditorium. That was God's work—no matter how I felt, He was there, holding me up and moving in His strength.

That afternoon, I rested, knowing that my God is faithful, never limited by our feelings or our expectations.

We all need to refuel sometimes, especially with something good and fiery—like hot sauce! Nothing like the hottest spice to wake up the senses. But in all seriousness, this story isn't just about physical

Vicki Jamison Peterson: God's Anointed Vessel

nourishment; it's about fueling ourselves with the strength and power of God's anointing.

In **Ephesians 6:13-14**, it says, ***"Wherefore take unto you the whole armour of God, that ye may be able to withstand in the evil day, and having done all, to stand. Stand therefore, having your loins girt about with truth, and having on the breastplate of righteousness"* (KJV)**. I had done all I knew to do. My life was in order, and I was doing my best to walk in the truth. But I still faced days where I needed more of God's presence to see me through. Sometimes it felt like I was barely hanging on.

During one of those hard times, I pushed myself to minister even though I didn't feel well. I noticed that as I operated under the anointing, my strength increased. So here's a little secret: stay close to the anointing. Get on the front row of God's work, so to speak. I learned that firsthand, sitting night after night under Kenneth Hagin's ministry, and one day, the anointing just fell on me, imparting the spiritual strength I needed.

By Tuesday of that week, even though I still felt weak, I had a determination not to give up. I remember that very night, a virus hit me suddenly—Satan's attempt to pull me down once again. But in God's grace, I woke up the next morning healed and filled with a strength that I know only came from the anointing. **Isaiah 10:27** tells us, ***"And it shall come to pass in that day, that his burden shall be taken away from off thy shoulder, and his yoke from off thy neck, and the yoke shall be destroyed because of the anointing."***

The Holy Spirit's anointing has the power to break any yoke of sickness, fear, or bondage. Just as I experienced healing, I want to encourage you to stand, to press forward under God's power, because in Him, the victory is already won.

"Leaving No Stone Unturned: Faith, Endurance, and Standing Firm in God's Word"

When trials came my way, I knew I had to stand firm on God's promises, holding tightly to His Word. James 1:22 says, *"**But be ye doers of the word, and not hearers only, deceiving your own selves**"* (KJV). I took this to heart, refusing to let circumstances or physical weakness dictate my life. I wasn't just hearing the Word—I was acting on it. God called me to preach the gospel, and I believed no institution, hospital, or nursing home would ever hold me. I've made a declaration that I won't be confined by illness, and I'll keep speaking and believing it, knowing that life and death are in the power of the tongue **(Proverbs 18:21).**

Yet, as the battles continued, the journey wasn't easy. After a time of great progress, I found myself spiraling down once more. I knew the Word was my stronghold, but it felt like everything was fighting to keep me from victory. **Hebrews 10:36** tells us, *"**For ye have need of patience, that, after ye have done the will of God, ye might receive the promise.**"* I resolved to push on.

During a particularly challenging week, Kenneth Hagin

Vicki Jamison Peterson: God's Anointed Vessel

held meetings, and I knew in my spirit that I had to attend. Despite feeling weak, I set out, determined to leave no stone unturned. I could have let excuses stop me, but I knew the Holy Spirit was urging me to be there. When I arrived, the anointing was so powerful, like crystal-clear water washing over me, and God's presence lifted my spirit. Brother Hagin ministered to me, reminding me, *"You're not finished yet."* God's words were like a lifeline, reminding me that I still had a purpose.

Encouraged and renewed, I committed to moving forward, even though it meant exercising my faith and my body to rebuild what had been broken. Each day I walked, sometimes staggering from dizziness, but I knew I was breaking through into the promise of healing and wholeness. I walked miles, pushing through physical pain to reach the other side of my healing.

"For we walk by faith, not by sight" (2 Corinthians 5:7), and through this, I learned the truth of that scripture like never before.

Faith is sometimes a journey through pain to reach the glory that God has promised. The Word of God teaches us to persevere, even when it means breaking through pain barriers. **Romans 5:3-4 says, *"And not only so, but we glory in tribulations also: knowing that tribulation worketh patience; And patience, experience; and experience, hope"* (KJV).** I knew I had to push through the challenges, not just pray for a quick miracle but fight my way back to health and strength.

At City of Faith, I'd walk laps on the track, wobbly at first, but I wouldn't quit. Eventually, I built up strength to run, even if it was just a few feet at a time. With the Word, with faith, and under the anointing, I ran until I made it through one lap, then two, then half a mile. Now, I'm aiming for a full mile without stopping. It's a miracle. I'm running for my life because I believe in God's promises, and I've seen Him work through every painful step.

Psalm 91:16 assures us, *"With long life will I satisfy him, and shew him my salvation."* Health doesn't simply fall on us, but it can be possessed, held onto with faith and persistence. Every step I took—no matter how painful—was a testimony that healing belongs to me. I refuse to settle for anything less than a full victory. God doesn't love me more than anyone else; He has this same promise for everyone who fights for it.

When doubts and symptoms reappear, I just laugh. I know that God has given me the tools to fight. I tell Satan, "You're wasting your time." I'm not just here to survive; I'm here to thrive. I'm glad my healing came this way because I have learned, grown, and built my faith in a way that only comes through persevering with God's strength. As James 1:2-3 encourages us, *"My brethren, count it all joy when ye fall into divers temptations; Knowing this, that the trying of your faith worketh patience."*

**"Unshaken Faith: Standing Firm in

Vicki Jamison Peterson: God's Anointed Vessel

God's Promise and Revelation"**

"God, who at sundry times and in divers manners spake in time past unto the fathers by the prophets, Hath in these last days spoken unto us by his Son, whom he hath appointed heir of all things, by whom also he made the worlds." (Hebrews 1:1-2)

God's heart is to work in and through His people, calling us into deeper communion with Him. Our journey with the Lord is marked by revelation—a personal, Spirit-led understanding that unveils truth step by step. The truth is that only through divine revelation do we truly come to know God. You can study scripture diligently and fill your mind with knowledge, but real understanding of Him, and a personal walk with Jesus, only comes by revelation through the Holy Spirit.

"No man can come to me, except the Father which hath sent me draw him..." (John 6:44). Revelation begins with our need for Him, as the Holy Spirit awakens us to see our emptiness without God. It's that inner conviction that drives us to seek Jesus as our Savior. The Spirit reveals God's love, showing us that no matter where we've come from or what we've done, there's hope in Him. He says to each of us, "Come to Me, for I am the Door. I am your only hope." Jesus welcomes all who turn to Him.

God wants you to know that you're not your own; you've been bought with a price and called to glorify Him.

"Know ye not that your body is the temple of the Holy Ghost which is in you, which ye have of God, and ye are not your own? For ye are bought with a price: therefore glorify God in your body, and in your spirit, which are God's" (1 Corinthians 6:19-20). Our bodies are His temple, purposed to honor Him, and through us, God's power and presence are displayed.

Let there be a demonstration of Christ's love, joy, and truth flowing through you, so evident that when people are around you, they sense the presence of Jesus. Not through mere talk, but through a life empowered by the Spirit. Let us fight the good fight of faith, leave no stone unturned, and declare: *"I will not be denied! I will not give up what belongs to me in Christ!"* Stand in faith, in His promise, and let His Spirit guide you each step of the way.

"All Things Belong to God: A Call to Surrender and Listen"

If you're caught up in personalities, you're missing the true message. Don't you see? Our lips, our feet, and these temples of flesh are just clay vessels—ordinary, fragile, finite. It's only when the fire of the Holy Spirit flows through us that these bodies become a demonstration of God's presence. *"**Know ye not that ye are the temple of God, and that the Spirit of God dwelleth in you?**"* **(1 Corinthians 3:16).** The only qualification you need is a body willing to let Him work through it.

Vicki Jamison Peterson: God's Anointed Vessel

"God, who at sundry times and in divers manners spake in time past unto the fathers by the prophets, Hath in these last days spoken unto us by his Son, whom he hath appointed heir of all things, by whom also he made the worlds" **(Hebrews 1:1-2).** For nearly 2,000 years, we've been in these "last days," and today we're in the "last of the last days." How do we know? The Spirit tells us, stirring the hearts of those prepared to meet the Lord. This Bride, the Church, is being made ready, clothed in righteousness and devotion to Him alone.

You might say, "I worked hard for everything I have. It's mine!" But, beloved, it all belongs to God. He is the rightful owner of all creation, and everything He has made is sustained by His hand. *"**For the earth is the Lord's, and the fulness thereof; the world, and they that dwell therein**"* **(Psalm 24:1)**. God, in His mercy, gives rain to the just and unjust alike simply because He loves us all.

As I walk through mountains and forests, taking in the beauty of the mountains and the peace of the trees, I'm reminded of how everything belongs to Him. Every stream, every creature, and every person reflects His creative hand. God will speak if we are willing to listen. In the peace of nature, in the stillness of our hearts, He speaks if we quiet ourselves before Him.

Are you ready to release everything into His hands, knowing that your life, breath, and every blessing come from Him? He is calling us to acknowledge that *"**the earth is the Lord's,"* and we are simply stewards, entrusted with what belongs to Him.

"All Things Belong to God: The Beauty of His Creation and Our Faith in Him"

Have you ever journeyed into the mountain ranges of Montana or walked through the breathtaking Sierra Nevada's? Underneath the rocks, you'll sometimes find a small pocket of bubbling, warm spring water, provided for thirsty creatures—deer, elk, bear, and fox. God, in His love, created such things to sustain even the smallest of His creatures. When spring brings the brilliant scarlet tanager with her vibrant reds and oranges, He guides her to create a home for her young. How perfectly He provides! As Scripture tells us, *"**Are not two sparrows sold for a farthing? and one of them shall not fall on the ground without your Father"*** (Matthew 10:29). If God so carefully provides for these, how much more does He care for you?

The Lord's creation is ordered by His mighty Word, not by accident or chance. **Hebrews 1:2-3 (KJV)** declares, *"**Hath in these last days spoken unto us by his Son, whom he hath appointed heir of all things, by whom also he made the worlds; Who being the brightness of his glory, and the express image of his person, and upholding all things by the word of his power."*** Jesus, the express image of the Father, sustains, maintains, and directs all of creation. And now He is

Vicki Jamison Peterson: God's Anointed Vessel

seated at the right hand of the Father, His work complete, having cleansed us from sin and guilt.

Each step in faith draws us closer to this fullness in Him. First, we come to salvation, then to the baptism of the Holy Spirit, and then to the beauty of being led by Him. *"For without faith it is impossible to please Him"* (Hebrews 11:6). God's ways may not always make logical sense to us; He calls us to believe and to obey, whether or not we understand. *"Whatsoever he saith unto you, do it"* (John 2:5). It is this childlike faith that allows us to enter into His complete provision and love.

When we recognize that everything belongs to God, we can trust that He knows our needs and will meet them. You don't have to leave tonight with any unmet need. He calls you to be filled, to know His peace, and to find rest in His love. He who sustains every creature in creation is surely more than able to care for you.

"Complete in Him: The Revelation of Faith and Wisdom"

In our journey with God, we find that *"without faith it is impossible to please him"* (Hebrews 11:6, KJV). God has so much more to reveal to us—He's more eager to bring us into His fullness than we are to receive it! How many of us long to know more of Him?

He has come to make us complete, and the work is already finished! Jesus, seated at the right hand of the Father, has accomplished everything needed for our spiritual completeness. What is He waiting on? He's waiting for us to step into that fullness. He's waiting for us to take hold of the promises He's already given.

Sometimes, we think that joining a particular church or following certain practices will bring us closer to God's perfection, only to find that there is no perfect church—because we are in it! Yet, God's love for us remains steadfast.

Let's turn our focus now to Colossians 1, where Paul's prayer for the church at Colossae extends to us today as the living Body of Christ. ***"For this cause we also, since the day we heard it, do not cease to pray for you, and to desire that ye might be filled with the knowledge of his will in all wisdom and spiritual understanding"*** **(Colossians 1:9, KJV).** This prayer of the Holy Spirit is a call to receive His fullness, not merely a beginning with salvation, but an invitation to be filled with a deep, clear understanding of God's will.

Paul's prayer goes beyond mere knowledge. He prays for us to gain a comprehensive insight into God's ways and purposes, a discernment of spiritual things that only comes from the Holy Spirit. This wisdom leads us to a deeper walk with God, revealing His heart and mind to us in a way that transforms our lives.

We are on a journey, friends. We haven't arrived yet, but we're on our way, filled with a purpose to grow in Him,

Vicki Jamison Peterson: God's Anointed Vessel

to gain spiritual insight, and to fulfill His will. And as we embrace each revelation, may we grow more complete in Him, strengthened in faith and filled with His wisdom.

God desires for each of us to understand His will. He wants us to be filled with His knowledge and to know His will for our lives. I often hear people say, "Oh, if I only knew the will of God!" But God wants you to know His will even more than you want to know it. And, thankfully, He has made His will available to us through His Word and by the guidance of the Holy Spirit.

People sometimes come to me and ask, "Will you pray with me about this?" I often respond, "No, I don't need to pray about that because I can already give you the answer." You see, the knowledge of His will is available to us in His Word. As we immerse ourselves in it, we find that God's will becomes clearer.

*"**For this cause we also, since the day we heard it, do not cease to pray for you, and to desire that ye might be filled with the knowledge of his will in all wisdom and spiritual understanding**"* (Colossians 1:9, KJV). God doesn't want you wandering in confusion. He provides wisdom and understanding as we draw close to Him.

The Holy Spirit speaks to our hearts, not our mind, guiding us with impressions and insights that align with His peace. When we feel a sense of joy or peace about a decision, it's often His affirmation. When there's a hesitation, that's His way of saying, "Hold back." It's important to listen to these promptings. If you ignore His voice, you may end up regretting it. Proverbs says, *"In all thy ways acknowledge him, and he shall direct thy paths"* (Proverbs 3:6, KJV).

Following God's will isn't about looking for big signs once in a while; it's a daily communion with Him. This walk with God is simpler than we sometimes make it. It's like any close relationship—you learn to recognize His voice, just as a child knows the voice of their parent. He's as close to us as any family member, and His voice becomes clearer as we spend time in His presence.

This life of walking with God is filled with surprises and beauty because it's a journey of faith. We may not know what He will do each day, but that's the excitement of walking with Him. Sometimes, He hides tomorrow's plans, not to keep us in the dark, but because He delights in revealing them at the right time. And He gives us the understanding we need when we need it.

God wants us to know His will—not just occasionally, but in the day-to-day details of our lives. Draw near to Him, and His guidance will come naturally, like a close friend walking by your side.

"Drawn into the Kingdom: Living in God's Authority and Rest"

Do you think God is a distant dictator, hearing us from a

Vicki Jamison Peterson: God's Anointed Vessel

far-off throne with no concern for our day-to-day needs? Not at all! He's with us each and every day, listening, leading, and caring for us personally. God said, *"I will never leave thee, nor forsake thee"* (Hebrews 13:5, KJV). He is right by your side, ready to meet every need, calm every worry, and lift every burden. He asks us not to be anxious because we belong to Him now, and as our Father, He takes full responsibility for us.

As believers, we are called to live as new creatures, to enter into His rest, and to reign with Christ. We're not just saved to follow along; we are invited to share in His authority and purposes! God wants us to understand this truth so deeply that it transforms our every action, decision, and relationship. *"And be renewed in the spirit of your mind"* (Ephesians 4:23, KJV). We are called into His peace, and in Christ, we're given new life and access to His authority.

God wants us to walk in full knowledge of His will, deeply rooted in spiritual wisdom. **Colossians 1:9** reminds us that Paul prayed for us to have a *"full, deep, and clear knowledge of His will in all wisdom and spiritual understanding."* God's desire is for us to know His heart and walk in discernment so that we recognize and follow His ways.

Verse 13 shows us God's work in our lives:

"Who hath delivered us from the power of darkness, and hath translated us into the kingdom of his dear Son" (Colossians 1:13, KJV).

Think of it! We are drawn by the Holy Spirit out of darkness and into the kingdom of light. If God is prompting you today, don't delay—move with Him! God is extending His arm, saying, "Come, I will heal you. I'll lift your burdens, give you clarity, and meet your needs." He's calling us out of darkness, not only to be free but to live in His kingdom under His authority.

And in this, we also have a part to play: speak His Word. When we remind Satan that we have been drawn out of his control and into the kingdom of God, we're standing firm in our identity and freedom in Christ. Remind the enemy, saying, "I have been drawn by the Father out of your dominion, and my body is the temple of the Holy Ghost. You have no place in me." As **James 4:7** teaches, *"**Submit yourselves therefore to God. Resist the devil, and he will flee from you.**"* This Word is our authority and our defense.

Finally, in verse 14, we read about this redemption:

*"**In whom we have redemption through his blood, even the forgiveness of sins**"* **(Colossians 1:14, KJV).**

Because of His love, we've been redeemed and forgiven. The Lord has transferred us from a place of sin to a place of grace, from bondage into freedom. Tonight, take hold of this truth—God has drawn you into His Kingdom, where He provides, protects, and reigns forever. Walk in the fullness of His calling and live under His authority and love.

Vicki Jamison Peterson: God's Anointed Vessel

DR MICAEL H YEAGER
AUTHORS SUPERNATURAL EXPERIENCE

How God Healed Me of Hernia

*I Kept Radically SHOVING my intestines back into where they belonged with my fingers for two weeks.

Day after day we were putting up the steel for our new church facility. We only had the use of the crane for one day. The crane had handled all the heaviest beams. All the rest of the steel had to be carried up to the top of the building and placed by hand. I'm not a very large man, as I only weighed about 140 pounds at the time. I was pulling and tugging, walking on steel beams, and balancing precariously with large steel purlins over my shoulder over 20 feet above the ground.

One day, as I was trying to put a heavy beam into place, I felt something rip in my lower abdomen. Later that day I noticed I had a small bulge in my abdomen area. I had torn loose some stomach muscles. I had a hernia! I did not tell anyone. I found a quiet place and cried out to God. I laid my hands over the hernia, commanding it to go in the name of Jesus Christ of Nazareth, and I went back to work because the building had to be put up.

Every day I kept on lifting heavy steel. The hernia did not go away so I kept looking to God, trusting, and believing. The only one who became aware of the hernia was my wife. Honestly, I do not even remember telling her.

Why would I not tell anyone? It wasn't because I was afraid that they would have a poor opinion of me because I wasn't getting healed. I've never worried in the least about people thinking I did not have faith. Faith is the substance that is or is not. The Bible says if any man has faith, let him have it to himself.

Romans 14:22 Hast thou faith? Have it to thyself before God.

In my heart, there was nothing I needed to prove to anyone, but to God himself. You see, my confidence is in Jesus Christ, the heavenly Father, and the Holy Ghost, and the Word of God! If I must go to the doctor, or use medication, it's nobody's business.

For over two years this hernia remained with me. I thought it was three, but my wife says it was two. Every time this hernia would bother me, I would lay hands over the top of it, and command it to go, thanking God that I was healed.

Eventually, this hernia began to get very serious. It began to bulge so far from my body that I knew eventually it would strangle. A strangled hernia is very dangerous.

A strangulated hernia is a hernia that cuts off the blood supply to the intestines and tissues in the abdomen. Symptoms of a strangulated hernia include pain near a hernia that gets worse very quickly and may be associated with other symptoms.

I knew in my heart that it was time to get very serious about this situation. You see the kingdom of heaven sufferings violence and the violent take it by force. I knew that I knew that I knew that by the stripes of Jesus I am healed. I literally began to take the fingers of my right

Vicki Jamison Peterson: God's Anointed Vessel

hand shoving this hernia back up into my stomach lining and speaking to my stomach lining and commanding it to be healed. For approximately two weeks I kept on aggressively shoving this hernia back into my body, declaring that it was healed.

In the world they say: it's the early bird that gets the worm. In Christianity: It's the Spiritually Violent Man That Gets the Answer.

Now, this type of faith needs to be developed. It's absolute unwavering, and total confidence, I cannot be defeated attitude and God.

Hebrews 6:18 that by two immutable things, in which it was impossible for God to lie, we might have a strong consolation, who have fled for refuge to lay hold upon the hope set before us:

I went to bed one night approximately two weeks after I had become aggressive with my faith in Christ and woke up the next morning to an amazing miracle. The hernia was completely gone. That was over 35 years ago, and it has never come back. Faith is the substance of things hoped for, the evidence of things not seen!

Michael H Yeager

CHAPTER EIGHT
"Walking in Authority: Reigning with Christ"

When you become saved, Satan loses his hold over you. Now, some may ask, "Does this mean I can't sin?" No, that's not what it means. It means the power of sin over you has been broken by faith in Jesus Christ. Romans, particularly chapters 3 and 6, explains this clearly, reminding us: ***"Neither yield ye your members as instruments of unrighteousness unto sin: but yield yourselves unto God, as those that are alive from the dead, and your members as instruments of righteousness unto God"*** (Romans 6:13, KJV).

This truth means that we are no longer bound by the power of darkness. You don't have to live defeated. The authority is now in your hands to live victoriously. This is part of the revelation God has for you as a believer—your power and authority in Christ. You are no longer

Vicki Jamison Peterson: God's Anointed Vessel

under sin's dominion; you now have the power to choose righteousness.

As a Christian, you hold more power than you might realize. Jesus said, *"Ye are the salt of the earth... Ye are the light of the world"* (Matthew 5:13-14, KJV). That's who you are. Through His Church, which is made up of believers like you and me, God will accomplish His purposes here on earth.

Until you understand the authority you have in Christ, you won't be able to walk in the fullness of what He has for you. You are called to reign with Him, to share His throne. So, I want you to look in the mirror and declare, "I share His throne. I share His authority. I reign with Christ. Satan will not have dominion over my life." Doesn't that lift your souls? That's the power of God's Word in action!

This truth might take time to fully settle in your heart, but as it does, you'll rise to experience the fullness of what God has for you.

Now, Colossians 1:15 reminds us of who Jesus is:

"Who is the image of the invisible God, the firstborn of every creature" (Colossians 1:15, KJV).

Jesus is the visible image of our invisible God, and we, as believers, are made to reflect His light. Let this truth strengthen you as you walk in your God-given authority, knowing that you are empowered to live a life of victory and purpose.

Did you know that you are the visible representation of the invisible Christ on this earth? Yes, *you* are! As a believer, you are the physical, tangible reflection of Jesus in the world today. That's why people feel drawn to you, why they reach out to you. They are seeking God, often without realizing it. But beware—never take this onto yourself or become prideful, for Scripture says, *"**I am the Lord: that is my name: and my glory will I not give to another, neither my praise to graven images**"* **(Isaiah 42:8, KJV)**. Jesus Himself said, *"**If I do not the works of my Father, believe me not**"* **(John 10:37, KJV)**. Even Christ, in all His glory, gave honor to the Father, so we must remember that the power working through us is not our own.

As part of His Church, we are called to do His works. Jesus spoke these powerful words in **John 14:12: *"Verily, verily, I say unto you, He that believeth on me, the works that I do shall he do also; and greater works than these shall he do; because I go unto my Father."*** He was talking about you! He wasn't just speaking to pastors or apostles, but to *anyone* who believes in Him. Through His Spirit, we are empowered to perform His works—yes, even miracles.

It's true that God has given the Church specific roles—apostles, prophets, pastors, teachers, and evangelists. As **Ephesians 4:11-12** says, *"**And he gave some, apostles; and some, prophets; and some, evangelists; and some, pastors and teachers; for the perfecting of the saints, for the work of the ministry, for the edifying of the body of Christ.**"* These roles equip the Church, but His

Vicki Jamison Peterson: God's Anointed Vessel

promise to do great works is for all believers.

As you grow in faith, there is a revelation that goes beyond salvation. You discover your place in Christ and come to understand your authority, your position in Him. Just as Jesus reigned, so are you called to reign with Him, for **Romans 5:17** says, *"For if by one man's offence death reigned by one; much more they which receive abundance of grace and of the gift of righteousness shall reign in life by one, Jesus Christ."*

Friend, you are called to walk in this authority. So, let's hold fast to His promise and walk as the visible image of Christ, knowing that we are empowered by His Spirit to do His works and bring His love to the world.

"Christ Revealed: Discovering His Wisdom, Power, and Authority in You"

Let's dive back into the book of Colossians, a powerful reminder of who Jesus is and who we are in Him. Colossians 1 speaks of Jesus as *"the image of the invisible God, the firstborn of every creature"* **(Colossians 1:15, KJV)**. Now, on this earth, **you** are called to be that visible representation of the invisible Christ! Through you, God desires to perform the mighty works that Christ did, even the "greater works" He promised. Let's read further:

> "For by him were all things created, that are in heaven, and that are in earth, visible and invisible, whether they be thrones, or dominions, or principalities, or powers: all things were created by him, and for him: And he is before all things, and by him all things consist" (Colossians 1:16-17, KJV).

Here, we see Jesus—the One by whom all things were created, the Head of His Body, the Church, the One who holds all things together. **Jesus** is His Name!

> "And he is the head of the body, the church: who is the beginning, the firstborn from the dead; that in all things he might have the preeminence" (Colossians 1:18, KJV).

He alone stands preeminent, first in everything. The fullness of God dwells in Him permanently, for it pleased the Father to make it so (Colossians 1:19). This is why we must come to know Jesus deeply.

Let's move to Colossians 2:3, which reveals even more:

> "In whom are hid all the treasures of wisdom and knowledge" (Colossians 2:3, KJV).

So, if all the treasures of divine wisdom and knowledge are hidden in Jesus, how do we access them? The answer is simple: **we must come to know Him**. Paul himself longed *"that I may know him"* (Philippians 3:10, KJV). Knowing Jesus is the key to unlocking the treasures of His wisdom, knowledge, and understanding.

Vicki Jamison Peterson: God's Anointed Vessel

When you build a relationship with Jesus, He reveals Himself to you, one revelation at a time. You begin to understand that He truly provides for all your needs, heals your every ailment, and carries every burden you cast upon Him. He is able to do all this and more!

As we become aware of this truth, we grow in our identity in Christ. We come to understand that we are called to walk in His authority, reflecting His wisdom and glory on earth. Jesus, the fullness of God, lives in you, and through you, God intends to demonstrate His love, power, and wisdom to a watching world. So, let us draw near, seeking to know Him deeply and to walk boldly as the visible reflection of the invisible Christ!

In John 16, we find Jesus, preparing His disciples for His departure, yet He shares a promise for all who follow Him:

> **"I have yet many things to say unto you, but ye cannot bear them now" (John 16:12, KJV).**

Jesus knew His disciples weren't ready to receive everything He wanted to teach. Similarly, He brings revelation into our lives as we're ready to receive it, one truth at a time. We're all on a journey of continuous learning, where Jesus speaks through His Word, guiding us by His Spirit, and providing for our every need.

As ministers, we feel this call to go wherever God leads, even here in Fresno, where we sense a deep hunger in your hearts—a longing for more of God, for victory, and for strength. When we arrive in a city, our hope is always to pour out as much as possible, leaving you more filled with faith and truth than before. We've seen lives transformed when people grasp these revelations. They rise up in strength, leave behind the things that held them back, and embrace their identity in Christ.

That's why we send out books, tapes, and monthly messages. It's about touching the Church with truth, helping the Body grow in revelation after revelation, to come fully into Christ's image and His purpose. Leaving isn't easy, knowing there's always more to share, more people to reach, more prayers to pray. But God orchestrates connections within His Body so that each person is reached, each need met, each heart encouraged. This unity is our purpose—there's no competition in Christ, only the working together for His Kingdom.

We each have a unique role, and every believer is essential. Just as God calls us to minister, He has a place and purpose for each of you in the Body of Christ. Seek Him, and He will reveal His path for you. As we each walk in the revelation He gives, we fulfill His call, making His Kingdom known here on earth.

"Growing in Revelation: The Spirit's Work in Us"

As Jesus prepared to leave His disciples, He expressed a powerful truth, saying:

Vicki Jamison Peterson: God's Anointed Vessel

> **"I have yet many things to say unto you, but ye cannot bear them now" (John 16:12, KJV).**

I can relate to His words in a small way. Each time I leave a town, I feel like there's more I wish I could share. But just as Jesus said, revelation comes when we're ready to receive it, and God gives it piece by piece. Growth in faith doesn't happen overnight. It's built **"line upon line, precept upon precept" (Isaiah 28:10).** We're drawn deeper by many separate revelations, where truth is added to truth, leading us to a fuller knowledge of God.

Jesus promised that we wouldn't be left on our own. He spoke these words of comfort:

> **"When he, the Spirit of truth, is come, he will guide you into all truth" (John 16:13, KJV).**

Jesus knew it was necessary for Him to go away so that the Holy Spirit could come, saying, **"I will not leave you comfortless" (John 14:18, KJV).** This was a promise of Pentecost. The Spirit of Truth would come to lead us into all truth, to be our Comforter and Guide, to reveal to us everything Jesus wants us to know.

When the Holy Spirit moves, He always leads us to see Jesus more clearly. In **John 16:14,** Jesus says of the Holy Spirit:

> **"He shall glorify me: for he shall receive of mine, and shall shew it unto you."**

The Holy Spirit's purpose is to glorify Jesus, to reveal more of Him to us, taking us from the foundation of salvation and leading us, step by step, into deeper revelations. Through the Spirit's guidance, we are transformed from glory to glory, becoming more complete in all God has for us.

We've learned that God wants us to know His will and His purpose for us. But this wisdom and knowledge are hidden in Christ, as Paul wrote:

> "In whom are hid all the treasures of wisdom and knowledge" (Colossians 2:3, KJV).

Yet God hasn't left us without a way to access this wisdom. He gave us the Holy Spirit as the means by which these hidden things are revealed. This is why we need the baptism of the Holy Spirit, to fully experience the revelations God has prepared for us.

As believers, we don't need to turn to any worldly sources to know God's purpose. The Holy Spirit is our guide and will reveal to us what we need to know, in God's timing and by His grace.

"The Power of His Word: From Death to Life"

Vicki Jamison Peterson: God's Anointed Vessel

The Word of God has an incredible power to heal, transform, and bring life in times of deepest need. Reflecting on Ezekiel 16:6, which says:

> **"And when I passed by thee, and saw thee polluted in thine own blood, I said unto thee when thou wast in thy blood, Live; yea, I said unto thee when thou wast in thy blood, Live" (KJV).**

I learned the life-saving power of these words firsthand. In Bible school, we were taught the significance of this scripture, and testimonies were shared of how it brought healing and restoration when spoken over those in critical condition. This verse became more than words on a page for me—it became a life source.

One day, I found myself in Methodist Hospital, barely hanging on due to blood clots that had nearly destroyed my lungs. I was on blood thinners, but my body was too frail, and I began to hemorrhage severely. Blood poured from my body in every way imaginable. The doctors worked tirelessly, administering transfusions, but nothing seemed to help. I was rapidly slipping away, with little strength or awareness remaining.

By evening, my condition hadn't improved. The curtain around my hospital bed seemed to signal a finality—curtains drawn, and whispers exchanged in somber tones. Yet, as the doctors stayed close, waiting for any sign of change, I became aware of a presence greater than any medical effort—the Holy Spirit, my Comforter and Standby. He spoke to my spirit in that quiet, yet unmistakable voice, reminding me of **Ezekiel 16:6.**

In a voice barely above a whisper, I called for my friend Joe. "Joe, get my Bible," I managed to say. She brought it and stood beside me, opening to the passage. As she read, **"And when I passed by thee, and saw thee polluted in thine own blood, I said unto thee when thou wast in thy blood, Live; yea, I said unto thee when thou wast in thy blood, Live,"** I held on to those words with my spirit, accepting them as God's living Word for me in that moment.

In faith, I received the power of that Word, and something miraculous happened. It felt as if life flowed into me. I began to sing the 23rd Psalm:

> **"The Lord is my shepherd; I shall not want. He maketh me to lie down in green pastures: he leadeth me beside the still waters. He restoreth my soul..." (Psalm 23:1-3, KJV).**

The strength of His Word brought peace and life into my soul. I believe now, more than ever, in the unshakable truth that His Word is alive and powerful, ready to bring life, healing, and restoration in our darkest moments.

"Healing in His Presence: Finding Faith, Peace, and Restoration"

I didn't have much strength, but I began singing, **"The Lord's my shepherd; I shall not want. He maketh me to lie down in green pastures: he leadeth me beside**

Vicki Jamison Peterson: God's Anointed Vessel

the still waters" (Psalm 23:1-2, KJV). People around me tried to quiet me, saying I was too weak to sing. But when you're reaching out for healing, you have to press on. So, I kept singing, my voice growing louder with each line.

As I sang, something powerful took place—I knew in my spirit that I was being healed. Within thirty minutes, the hemorrhaging stopped entirely, and I never needed another blood transfusion. His promise held true: **"Peace I leave with you, my peace I give unto you" (John 14:27, KJV).** That peace flooded over me as my healing took place, and I felt the infinite love of God comforting me, reaching deeper than any words could describe.

In that moment, I sensed His presence so strongly, and I knew that His love was pouring out not just for me, but for everyone willing to receive it. If you're listening today, know this: God loves you deeply, individually. No matter how broken you may feel or how disfigured by life's struggles, God sees you as His beloved child, and He takes joy in you.

Later, God used me to minister healing to others. I was blessed to meet people like Joe and Erica from Spokane, Washington. Erica had been in severe pain with a degenerative issue between the fifth and sixth cervical vertebrae. Doctors recommended intricate surgery, but she believed God would heal her. During a service, I called out a healing for neck pain, but Erica hesitated until the Spirit nudged her, reminding her to claim her healing.

As she stepped forward in faith, her pain disappeared. She shared how she celebrated her birthday pain-free, and five years later, she still hadn't felt a single pain in her neck. God's faithfulness remains, and His healing power stands firm.

Each healing, each step of faith, each declaration of His promises brings us closer to His heart, where we find that His glory and love surround us. Jesus promised, "I am come that they might have life, and that they might have it more abundantly" (John 10:10, KJV).

DR MICAEL H YEAGER
AUTHORS SUPERNATURAL EXPERIENCE

"Miraculous Redemption: Connie's Journey from Atheism to Faith"

In the midst of our journey through life, we often encounter individuals whose stories resonate deeply within our hearts. Such was the tale of Connie, relayed to me by her devoted sister, Vicki. A tale where darkness collided with the divine light, where hope emerged from despair, and where God's unwavering love transformed an unbelieving heart.

Vicki, with tear-filled eyes and a heavy heart, frequently approached me with concerns about her sister. Connie was not merely an atheist, but her recent dalliance with Satanic rituals had left her tormented, perhaps even

Vicki Jamison Peterson: God's Anointed Vessel

demonized. To add to her affliction, she was grappling with severe physical ailments. Vicki's desperate pleas for her sister's salvation echoed in our sanctuary after every service. With hands joined, we implored the Lord for His divine intervention.

One evening, a deep-seated conviction gripped me: if the Almighty didn't step in swiftly, Connie's soul would be lost forever, and her life might tragically be cut short. Motivated by this divine nudge, I urged Vicki to intensify her prayers, promising my own fervent supplications alongside hers. Though Connie had been a faceless name to me, the Lord had planted her image deep within my spirit.

The next Sabbath, I felt led to encourage Vicki to bring Connie to our congregation. I believed that if Connie could journey from West Virginia to our sanctuary, the Almighty would enact a breathtaking transformation in her life. Despite Vicki's insistent pleas, Connie remained resistant, reluctant to step into our house of worship.

However, life took a grim turn. Vicki soon relayed that Connie was hospitalized, needing surgery. Amidst her hospital stay, she contracted a deadly strain of infection called MRSA - methicillin-resistant Staphylococcus aureus. This resilient "staph" bacteria often resists many of the antibiotics typically effective against staph infections. Such infections, once they enter the body, can wreak havoc, traveling to vital organs and bones. Tragically, every year, approximately 90,000 Americans grapple with this invasive menace, with nearly 20,000 succumbing to it.

Connie's condition deteriorated rapidly. To combat the fierce infection, doctors implanted a stint in her chest, delivering potent antibiotics directly into her primary arteries. Post-hospitalization, even the CDC got involved, with doctors paying regular visits to ensure her recovery. Amidst this tumultuous storm, in His mysterious ways, the Spirit of the Lord began to soften Connie's heart. She expressed a longing to attend our service, seeking prayer, regardless of her frail condition.

On an ordained Sunday, Vicki, Linda, and a frail Connie entered our sanctuary. As they stepped in, the palpable presence of God overwhelmed them. Vicki narrated how the atmosphere was so spiritually charged that tears streamed down many faces, including hers and Linda's. The congregation was deep in prayer and worship, with the Holy Spirit's presence overshadowing even my sermon.

Connie, amidst this spiritual downpour, was having her own encounter. The atheistic beliefs she had held onto began to dissolve. With eyes shut and heart open, she heard a commanding voice: "Get on Your Knees." Hesitation gripped her, for both her kneecaps had been replaced with metal. Yet, the voice persisted, compelling her to kneel. As she obeyed, she felt a hand upon her, initially thinking it to be mine. However, Vicki confirmed that no human hand had touched her. We firmly believe it was none other than Jesus Christ Himself, healing her broken body, casting out the tormenting spirits, and infusing her with divine life.

The evidence of her miraculous encounter was evident. Not only did Connie leave the church without her cane,

Vicki Jamison Peterson: God's Anointed Vessel

but her subsequent medical tests astounded the doctors. Nine tests were conducted, each failing to detect the previously rampant MRSA infection. The medical community was baffled, but we knew: Connie had experienced a touch from the Great Physician.

That day, the atheistic heart found solace in the Savior. Connie's spirit was rejuvenated, her body healed, and she was filled with the Holy Ghost. It was an awe-inspiring testimony of how God can rescue, heal, and deliver, even from the darkest pits. For as it is written in **Psalms 34:17-18 (KJV): "The righteous cry, and the LORD heareth, and delivereth them out of all their troubles. The LORD is nigh unto them that are of a broken heart; and saveth such as be of a contrite spirit."**

In Connie's story, we are reminded of the boundless mercy of Jesus, and the deceitful snares of the devil, Satan. But in the end, it is the power of Jesus Christ that prevails, providing hope and salvation to those who seek Him.

CHAPTER NINE
"Standing in Righteousness: Praying the Word with Authority"

Jesus came to redeem us, taking upon Himself all our sins and offering us His righteousness. On the cross, He exchanged His purity for our guilt, so that now, through Him, we are made righteous. As it says in **2 Corinthians 5:21, *"For he hath made him to be sin for us, who knew no sin; that we might be made the righteousness of God in him"* (KJV).** Understanding this is essential because, without it, we cannot stand in confidence against the devil. Our strength doesn't come from our own righteousness but from Christ's righteousness that we wear.

In **Ephesians 1:17-22**, Paul prays for believers to gain spiritual wisdom and knowledge, so they understand that the enemy is beneath the feet of Jesus. As part of His body, we too have that authority over the enemy, but knowledge of this truth is essential to living in that victory. Being in the kingdom of God does not shield us from challenges but equips us with a spiritual awareness to discern between good and evil.

Vicki Jamison Peterson: God's Anointed Vessel

Ephesians 6:17-18 instructs us to take up **"the helmet of salvation, and the sword of the Spirit, which is the word of God" (KJV),** while praying always with all kinds of prayer. Here, "word" refers to the Greek word *rhema*, which can imply a spoken or specific, personal word of God. When we place God's promises deep in our spirit, the Holy Spirit can bring them to our remembrance at just the right time, especially in moments of need. That's why it's so powerful to declare, *"**The Lord is my shepherd; I shall not want"*** **(Psalm 23:1, KJV),** because these words become alive, meeting our needs in every season.

Through His Word, we have been given all we need to stand in righteousness, equipped and ready to overcome.

I once witnessed an incredible miracle involving a woman who must've been about seventy years old. She came into one of my services, somewhere back in Tennessee or Kentucky, with her nose bandaged, bleeding from an aggressive cancer that had eaten away her skin. Despite her physical condition, her faith was rock-solid. She wouldn't be denied her healing—much like the paralyzed man let down through the roof to reach Jesus. Even though we tried to send her back, as I hadn't called for a specific healing at that moment, she wouldn't listen. She sat as close as she could, holding on to her faith.

Finally, as the Spirit led, I declared, "A nose is being healed now." I hadn't seen her yet, but as soon as I spoke those words, she took it as her sign. This little lady ran to the front, tore off the blood-soaked bandage, and it was a sight I'll never forget. The blood sprayed, and her nose was raw and deteriorated. But then, before everyone present, I saw something remarkable. Time itself seemed to slow, and her nose began to re-form right before our eyes. I watched it take shape, new skin appearing like that of a newborn. Her healing was instant and complete, a true creative miracle from the Holy Spirit. And after all that, she was the first to respond to the altar call, giving her life to Jesus with a face restored by God's power. As Scripture reminds us, *"**For with God nothing shall be impossible**"* (Luke 1:37, KJV).

In the mid-1990s, God led me to minister regularly at a small church in Ozark, Alabama, where I witnessed unique miracles and an outpouring of supernatural joy. With excitement, I'd often tell people, "Get on a plane, get on a train, get in a car—just come to the bar in Ozark, Alabama!" The Holy Spirit's presence was so evident that people left changed, even if they didn't feel it immediately. Sometimes, it wasn't even about what I said; it was simply about making space for the Spirit to move.

The anointing flows in various ways through different individuals, each bringing a unique impartation. As Paul wrote, *"**Now there are diversities of gifts, but the same Spirit**"* (1 Corinthians 12:4, KJV). When you receive from the Spirit, you are transformed—whether you realize it instantly or not. So keep seeking, keep pressing in, and open yourself up to all God has to offer.

Vicki Jamison Peterson: God's Anointed Vessel

"The Power of Joy and Faith: Opening Doors for God's Work in You"

There are times when I may appear to be waiting, but I know exactly what I'm doing. I'm waiting because I know we have the door of your heart open, and I know God can work deeply within you. It's not always about the words being spoken, but about creating space for the anointing, which brings the exact nourishment your soul needs. You see, joy in God's presence is wonderful, but there's more to it. We experience that joy to be strengthened for the challenges outside these walls. ***"For the joy of the LORD is your strength"* (Nehemiah 8:10, KJV).**

When you go back to the real world, sometimes the laughter fades and the weight of life presses in. You might even feel frustrated and wonder about the value of joy in church when trials come. But the purpose of this joy, this outpouring, is to open the windows of heaven long enough for God to fill you so completely that when trouble comes, you're fortified. ***"Consider it all joy, my brethren, when ye fall into divers temptations"* (James 1:2, KJV).** And you know what happens? You find that your cries in hardship become quieter, shorter, as your faith grows stronger.

That's the purpose here to let God's joy infuse you so deeply that your faith becomes unwavering. When joy leads you back to His Word, it becomes active and alive, sharper than a two-edged sword. *"**For the word of God is quick, and powerful, and sharper than any twoedged sword**"* **(Hebrews 4:12, KJV).** This joy and faith together make us victorious in Him.

So let the joy of the Lord flow, because *"the windows of heaven are open, and the blessings are falling"* tonight! Let us sing with hearts full of joy and faith, letting the world see Jesus in us. With joy and the Word, there is nothing the world can do to keep us down. We are overcomers through Him who loved us.

****"Victory Over Depression: A Mother's Journey to Healing"****

Women's testimony: When I was six years old, my beautiful mother, who is here with us today, went through a very difficult time. She had an emotional and mental breakdown. In the years that followed, there were more breakdowns due to the overwhelming pressures of life, which she didn't know how to cope with. Mother, would you come up here, please? Let's welcome my mother, Ruth Lamb, from Dallas, Texas.

Ruth: Thank you. The doctors could do very little for me. They gave me sleeping pills and told me to rest, but it didn't help. I suffered from deep depression that would last for days on end. My nerves were so frayed that I even contemplated suicide. The only thing that kept me going was looking at my small children. I felt that they were the reason I had to live. But it was a constant

Vicki Jamison Peterson: God's Anointed Vessel

struggle, and I felt like I was losing the battle for many, many years.

Even though I regained some physical and emotional stability, there would still be times of intense depression. The doctors had told me that my nerves were like a rubber band that had lost all of its elasticity—there was no hope for me. Then, I heard a woman from South Africa speak, and she was such a blessing. She taught that we must forget the past. I realized that I was condemning myself and carrying a heavy load of guilt. I had to learn to forgive and love myself, understanding that the things in the past were forgiven by God. If He had forgotten them, why should I keep remembering them?

One night, I went to bed but couldn't sleep. Around 11:30, I sat up and realized I had to do something. I took the Word of God—something I should have done much earlier—and wielded it like the sword of the Spirit. I began declaring, "Satan, I resist you in the name of Jesus. Take your hand off my body. I belong to God. I will forget those things which are behind, and I will press toward the goal." I stood on the promise in **Isaiah 53:5 (KJV): "But he was wounded for our transgressions, he was bruised for our iniquities: the chastisement of our peace was upon him; and with his stripes, we are healed."**

I repeated these declarations over and over. Just before midnight, I experienced the greatest victory of my life. It felt as if I had been cleansed anew; the depression lifted and was completely gone. Praise God, it has never returned.

Vicki: Isn't that marvelous? God truly sets us free.

This testimony reminds us of the power of God's Word to bring healing and deliverance. Ruth's story echoes the Apostle Paul's words in **Philippians 3:13-14 (KJV): "Brethren, I count not myself to have apprehended: but this one thing I do, forgetting those things which are behind, and reaching forth unto those things which are before, I press toward the mark for the prize of the high calling of God in Christ Jesus."**

When we hold fast to God's promises and resist the enemy in the name of Jesus, we can overcome the battles that seem insurmountable. Ruth's victory over depression is a testament to the transformative power of God's Word and His ability to restore hope and joy in our lives. No matter what we have faced, we can find healing and a new beginning in Christ. Let this story encourage you to take up the sword of the Spirit, the Word of God, and claim victory in every area of your life.

"The Mercy of God: A Journey from Blindness to Healing"

Vicki: I have a letter here from a doctor in Chicago, addressed to Mrs. Burton. Is that correct?

Vicki Jamison Peterson: God's Anointed Vessel

Mrs. Burton: Yes, I am Mrs. Burton.

Vicki: Would you kindly come up here and read this letter for us?

Mrs. Burton: Certainly. *[Reads the letter]* "Dear Mrs. Burton, this letter will certify that you are under my care for multiple sclerosis. This illness has rendered you legally blind. Your visual acuity was 2/400 in the left eye, and you are only able to count fingers with the right eye. Due to your visual disturbance, coordination issues, and weakness, your handwriting changes from time to time. You may use this letter to certify the above." It is signed by my doctor.

Vicki: Now, tell us what has happened to you since, and how did it all unfold?

Mrs. Burton: A year ago, I attended your crusade here in Chicago. I came with my husband and two children, not expecting to be healed. In fact, I wasn't born again and didn't even believe in what was happening. I didn't receive a healing the first night, the second night, or even that Sunday. In fact, I got worse—my eyes were badly infected.

When I returned home, my husband covered my "good" eye, the one that was legally blind, and left the completely blind eye uncovered. I happened to have a little Bible by my bedside. Usually, I used a talking book machine to read to me. But this time, I picked up the Bible and glanced down, and to my surprise, I started reading with my blind eye. Even then, I didn't fully believe it was real. My husband was very excited, but I was still doubtful.

Over the course of three months, I continued to improve. I eventually gave away my electric bed, wheelchair, and moped. Here I am today, walking and seeing quite well. I still have a little trouble with one eye, but I am so much better.

Vicki: So, the healing didn't occur during the service itself; it began that night and continued over a period of three months.

Mrs. Burton: That's right, it was a process.

Vicki: And you didn't even believe in it at first?

Mrs. Burton: No, I didn't.

Vicki: That's the mercy of God! Truly, it is all Jesus.

This testimony is a powerful reminder of God's mercy and His ability to heal, even when our faith seems small or absent. As **Psalm 103:2-3 (KJV)** declares, **"Bless the Lord, O my soul, and forget not all his benefits: Who forgiveth all thine iniquities; who healeth all thy diseases."** Mrs. Burton's journey demonstrates that God's healing touch is not confined to a moment; sometimes, it unfolds gradually as we continue to trust in His promises.

Vicki Jamison Peterson: God's Anointed Vessel

The fact that Mrs. Burton began reading with her blind eye is a testament to God's power to restore sight, fulfilling the words of **Isaiah 42:16 (KJV): "And I will bring the blind by a way that they knew not; I will lead them in paths that they have not known: I will make darkness light before them, and crooked things straight."** Her healing may not have happened instantaneously, but it was a miracle nonetheless, showcasing the compassion and mercy of our Lord.

God's healing power is not limited by our level of belief. His grace is often greater than our doubts, and His mercy reaches us in our weakest moments. Mrs. Burton's testimony serves as a beautiful illustration of how God's love works beyond our expectations, bringing hope and healing even when we least anticipate it. Let this story encourage you to trust in the Lord's goodness and to never underestimate the power of His mercy at work in your life.

"It's a New Day: From Reluctance to Obedience"

we have a testimony featuring a happy woman named Re Gray, who will share insights about some of the plants surrounding us—how to pot them, plant them, and even how they can relate to your spiritual life. So, stay tuned for what's sure to be an enriching experience.

Back in 1973, Vicki launched a women's television program on CBN called *It's a New Day.* She produced and hosted the half-hour show, featuring guests such as Kenneth and Gloria Copeland, Kathryn Kuhlman, and many other well-known figures in the Christian community. Later, in 1982, she began another broadcast called *Vicki Live,* which aired in Tulsa and New England.

Vicki: I want to tell you a story. I like "Once Upon a Time" tales, and this one is a story that will impact you for the rest of your life. Many years ago, I found myself in Methodist Hospital, but it wasn't just a hospital stay. In truth, I was running from the call of God. He had called me into ministry, but I wanted nothing to do with becoming a minister. It was the last thing on my mind. Yet, I found myself at a crossroads where I had to choose between obeying the Lord and using the Word I had learned, or continuing to run.

Let me take you back to my school days at Christ for the Nations. I was a first-year student, part of a group of about 40. We called ourselves "God's ragtag" because we were such a diverse bunch. There was an 80-year-old retired schoolteacher, a hippie who had just come off drugs and was still a bit spacey, and then there was me. No one took me seriously. They thought I was just a woman trying to fill time, unaware that God was working on my heart, calling me to learn His Word. At the time, I never planned on becoming a minister.

Vicki Jamison Peterson: God's Anointed Vessel

After that, I began to minister alongside Kenneth and Aretha Hagin, traveling with them. But even then, I was still reluctant to fully step into the ministry God had called me to. One of the teachers at Christ for the Nations was Mama Goodwin, who, along with her husband, taught us valuable lessons. She would often refer to a passage from Ezekiel, which became a foundation for my journey.

Ezekiel 16:6 (KJV) says, "And when I passed by thee, and saw thee polluted in thine own blood, I said unto thee when thou wast in thy blood, Live; yea, I said unto thee when thou wast in thy blood, Live." That verse spoke to me about God's power to bring life and healing where there seems to be no hope. It was as if God was saying to me, **"You may feel unqualified, reluctant, or even unwilling, but I have called you to live and to minister My Word."**

Through Vicki's story, we see the profound truth that God often calls us when we feel least prepared or willing. Like Vicki, many of us may hesitate to step into our calling, but God's grace enables us to fulfill His purposes. As **Isaiah 55:11 (KJV)** reminds us, **"So shall my word be that goeth forth out of my mouth: it shall not return unto me void, but it shall accomplish that which I please, and it shall prosper in the thing whereto I sent it."**

No matter where you are in life, if God is calling you,

His Word will accomplish His purposes. It may be a process, and you may have to wrestle with reluctance, but His plans for you are perfect and will bring you to a place of true fulfillment and joy. Let Vicki's story encourage you to trust in the Lord's calling, knowing that He equips those whom He calls.

DR MICAEL H YEAGER
AUTHORS SUPERNATURAL EXPERIENCE

(From the Book: Living In The Realm of the Miraculous)

My Amazing Supernatural Salvation

It was my nineteenth birthday (February 18, 1975). I was in the Navy at the time and heavily involved in alcohol, drugs, and other ungodly activities. I had decided to commit suicide. I do not remember anyone ever sharing the gospel of Jesus Christ with me. No one ever took the time to warn me about eternal damnation for those who did not know God. Even to this day it amazes me that the government ever accepted me into the Navy (back in 1973 when I was 17 years old). At the time I had major mental, emotional and even physical problems which included hearing problems and a major speech impediment. I quit school at 15 years old, leaving home until I ended up in trouble with the law at 16.

Vicki Jamison Peterson: God's Anointed Vessel

I was given the option of being prosecuted or joining the military. I chose the military. However, for the military to accept me, I had to have my GED. Subsequently, I worked extremely hard to get it and I succeeded. At the time, I really believed that joining the Navy would take me out of the drugs, violence, immorality, and alcohol lifestyle that I had been living. That could not have been farther from the truth.

As soon as I graduated from basic training, Uncle Sam shipped me to San Diego, California for further training on repairing 16mm projectors. Upon accomplishing this training, I was sent to Adak, Alaska in the Aleutian Islands. I was assigned to the special services department. They provided all of the entertainment for the men on base. This included the movie theater, bowling alley, roller-skating rink, horse stables for taking men hunting and the cafeteria (not the chow hall).

I was extremely unreliable and incompetent, so much so that within the two years that I was there, I was transferred to every one of those facilities. My last job ended up being at the horse stables shoveling manure. During this time I was heavily involved in drugs, including selling them. I was drinking a lot of alcohol including ripple wine, vodka and tequila. I smoked an average of 3 1/2 packs of cigarettes per day, not including cigars. I used Brown Mule, Copenhagen, Beach Nut, and Skoal chewing tobacco. My favorite singing groups were Dr. Hook and the Medicine Band, Pink Floyd, The Grateful Dead and America.

When I was off duty, my attire was extremely strange. First off, when I was younger, my older brother knocked out my front tooth. Of course, I had it replaced with a pegged tooth but while I was stationed in Adak, it got knocked out again. As a result, I picked up a ridiculous nickname. I was called "Tooth". I wanted to fit in with the cowboy crowd, so I found an old cowboy hat which was way too large for me. In order to make it fit, I took an old military ski hat and sewed it on the inside in order that it would be snug on my head. (Of course, this old Stetson cowboy hat was way too large for me.) As I would walk around the base with this large cowboy hat, it would be flopping on top of my head, making me look extremely silly; especially with me missing one of my front teeth.

I did not want to just be a cowboy because I was also a hippie. So, with a bright new idea, I went to the cafeteria and asked for all of their chicken necks. I took these chicken necks and boiled them in a pot of hot vinegar water. Then I took these chicken bones after they were cleaned and strung them on a leather strand. I would wear these chicken bones as a necklace around my neck. It really stank! No wonder I was extremely depressed all of the time.

I think that you can begin to see what kind of a mess I was. **However, supernaturally one night, God stepped into my life, instantly and radically changing me forever!** My last three months of military life was so amazingly transformed that I was put in charge of working parties and details from time to time. God instantly delivered me from all of my devices including all of my foolish behaviors. I was a new creature in Christ! Christ had supernaturally set me free from the tormenting demonic powers that had possessed my life for so long!

On my **19th birthday** I was overwhelmed with self-pity and depression. I decided to end it all by slitting my wrist! I went into the bathroom with a large, survival hunting knife. I put the knife to my wrist with the full intentions of slitting my artery. I was determined to kill myself. I held the knife firmly against my wrist and took one more last breath before I slid it across my wrist. Suddenly, an invisible presence came rushing down upon me like a blanket. It was a tangible, overwhelming presence of mind-boggling fear. It was the fear of God, and it overwhelmed me! Instantly, I realized with crystal-clear understanding that I was going to hell. I deserved hell; I belonged in hell, and hell had a right to me. Furthermore, I knew if I slit my wrist, I would be in hell forever.

And great fear came upon all the church, and upon as many as heard these things (Acts 5:11).

Overwhelming Love

I walked out of that little military bathroom to my bunk. I fell on my knees, reached my hands up toward heaven and cried out to Jesus with all of my heart. All of this was supernatural and strange. I did not ever recall any time when anyone ever shared with me how to become a Christian or how to be converted. Yet, I knew how to pray. I cried out to Jesus and told Him I believed He was the Son of God, had been raised from the dead, and I desperately needed Him.

I not only asked Him into my heart, but I gave Him my heart, soul, mind, and life. At that very instant, a love beyond description came rushing into my heart. I really knew what love was for the first time in my life. At the same time, I comprehended what I was placed on this earth for—I was here to follow, love, serve, and obey God. A deep love and hunger to know God grabbed my heart. I was filled with love from top to bottom, inside and out—inexpressibly beyond belief. Jesus had come to live inside of me!

Rivers of waters run down mine eyes, because they keep not thy law (Psalm 119:136).

Instantaneous Deliverance

I was instantly delivered: from over three packs of cigarettes a day, from worldly and satanic music, from chewing tobacco; from cussing and swearing, from drugs and alcohol, and from a filthy and dirty mind.

Some might ask why my conversion was so dramatic. I believe that it's because I had nothing to lose. I knew down deep that there was not one single thing worth saving in me. The only natural talent I ever possessed was the ability to mess things up. At the moment of salvation, I completely surrendered my heart and life to

Vicki Jamison Peterson: God's Anointed Vessel

Jesus Christ.

I am crucified with Christ: nevertheless I live; yet not I, but Christ liveth in me: and the life which I now live in the flesh I live by the faith of the Son of God, who loved me, and gave himself for me (Galatians 2:20).

OBSESSED WITH A DEEP HUNGER for GOD'S WORD!

I remember after giving my heart to **Jesus Christ** that I got up from the floor born again, saved and delivered, I was a brand-new person. Immediately hunger and thirst for the Word of God took a hold of me. I began to devour Matthew, Mark, Luke, and John. I just could not get enough of the word of God because of my love for **Jesus Christ** and his **Father**. **Jesus** became my hero in every area of my thoughts and daily life. He became my reason for getting up and going to work, eating, sleeping, and living.

I discovered that everything I did was based on the desire of wanting to please Him. I carried my little green military Bible with me wherever I went. Whenever I had an opportunity, I would open it up and study it. It wasn't very long before I believed for a larger Bible. This larger Bible gave me much more room to make notes, highlight and circle certain Scriptures. The more I fed on the Scriptures, the greater my hunger became for them. I probably was not saved even for 2 months when I was asked to speak for the 1st time at a small Pentecostal church. I believe it was called Adak Full Gospel Church.

As far as I know it was the only Pentecostal church on this military base situated on a Aleutian Island in Alaska. Since 1975 I have never lost my hunger, or my thirst for God's word. I can truly say even what the psalmist said!

Psalm 104:34 My meditation of him shall be sweet: I will be glad in the Lord.

CHAPTER TEN
Healed Me of Being Tongue-Tied!

After I gave my heart to **Christ** a divine hunger and thirst for the Word of God began to possess me. I practically devoured Matthew, Mark, Luke, and John. **Jesus** became my hero in every sense of the word, in every area of my thoughts and daily living. He became my soul reason for getting up every day and going to work, eating, sleeping, and living. I discovered that everything I did was based on a desire of wanting to please Him.

One day I was reading my Bible and discovered where **Jesus** said that it was necessary for him to leave. That because when he would go back to the **Father**, he would send the promise of the Holy Ghost to make us a witness. Furthermore, I learned it was His will for me to be filled to overflowing with the Holy Ghost and that the Holy Ghost would empower and equip me to be a witness an ambassador for God. The Holy Ghost would also lead me and guide me into all truth.

With all my heart I desperately wanted to reach the lost for **Jesus Christ** for they could experience the same love and freedom that I was now walking in. I searched the Scriptures to confirm this experience. In the book of Joel, in the old covenant, the four Gospels and especially in the book of acts I discovered the will of God when it comes to this baptism. I perceived in my heart that I needed to receive this baptism the same way that I had received salvation.

I had to look to **Christ** and trust by faith that he would give to me this baptism of the Spirit. It declared in the book of acts that after they were baptized in the Holy Ghost they all began to speak in a heavenly language. I had not been around what we would call Pentecostal people, so I had never heard anybody else speak in this heavenly language. But that did not really matter to me, because it was within the Scriptures.

Acts 2:39 For the promise is unto you, and to your children, and to all that are afar off, even as many as the Lord our God shall call.

I remember getting on my knees next to my bunk bed where I cried out and asked God to fill me with the Holy Ghost, so I could be a witness. As I was crying out to God something began to happen on the inside of me. It literally felt like hot buckets of oil were beginning to be poured upon me and within me. Something then began to rise out of my innermost being. Before I knew what I was doing, a new language came out bubbling of my mouth which I had never heard before or been taught to speak. I began to speak in a heavenly tongue.

Vicki Jamison Peterson: God's Anointed Vessel

Now up to this time I had a terrible speech impediment. You see I was born tongue-tied. Yes, they had operated on me, and I had gone to speech therapy, and yet most people could not understand what I was saying. I could not even pronounce my own last name YEAGER properly. My tongue simply refused to move in a way in which I could pronounce my Rs.

After I was done praying in this new language, I discovered to my absolute surprise that my speech impediment was instantly and completely gone! From that time on, I have never stopped preaching **Jesus Christ**. For almost 40 years I have proclaimed the truth of **Jesus Christ** to as many as I can.

And they were all filled with the Holy Ghost, and began to speak with other tongues, as the Spirit gave them utterance (Acts 2:4).

If I Was, I Am, If I Am, I Is!

While reading my Bible as a brand-new believer, (1975) I discovered that Jesus Christ went about healing ALL who were sick and oppressed of the devil. I began to search the Scriptures on this subject, and as I studied I discovered many Scriptures that support this:

Surely he hath borne our griefs, and carried our sorrows: yet we did esteem him stricken, smitten

of God, and afflicted. But he was wounded for our transgressions, he was bruised for our iniquities: the chastisement of our peace was upon him; and with his stripes we are healed (Isaiah 53:4-5).

Who his own self bare our sins in his own body on the tree, that we, being dead to sins, should live unto righteousness: by whose stripes ye were healed.1 Peter 2:24

When the even was come, they brought unto him many that were possessed with devils: and he cast out the spirits with his word, and healed all that were sick: That it might be fulfilled which was spoken by Esaias the prophet, saying, Himself took our infirmities, and bare our sicknesses. Matthew 8:16-17

As I read and meditated upon these Scriptures, something wonderful happened within my heart. Great, overwhelming sorrow took a hold of me as I saw the pain and the agony that Jesus went through for my healing. In my heart and in my mind, I saw that Jesus had taken my sicknesses and my diseases. I then experienced a great love for the son of God and recognize the price he paid for my healing.

When God gave me this revelation, revealed to me by the Scriptures, I experienced a great an overwhelming love for the son of God, recognizing the price he had paid for my healing. It was like an open vision in which I saw my precious **Lord and Savior** tied to the whipping post. I saw the Roman soldiers striking, beating, and whipping

Vicki Jamison Peterson: God's Anointed Vessel

the back of Jesus with the cat of nine tails. This was a Roman whip which had nine long strands, coated with oil, and covered with glass, metal shards, and sharp objects. In this vision I saw the flesh and the blood of my precious Savior splashing everything within a 10-foot radius, with each terrible stroke of the Romans soldier's whip hitting his body.

As I saw this open vision, (as I was on my knees in prayer) I wept because I knew that this horrendous beating he was enduring was for my healing, and my deliverance. To this day, even after 40 years, whenever I retell this story, great love, and sorrow still fills my heart for what Christ had to endure for me. This is the reason why I am so aggressive in my fight to receive healing. Still I have great joy, wonderful peace, and enthusiasm in this battle, because I know that by the **stripes of Jesus Christ I am healed**. This amazing price that he paid (God in the flesh) was not only for me, but for every believer who has received Christ as their Lord and Savior.

In this moment of this vision something exploded within my heart, an amazing faith possessed me with the knowledge that I no longer have to be sick. In the name of Jesus for over 40 years I have refused to allow what my precious Lord went through to be for nothing. I have refused to allow sickness and disease to dwell in my body, which is the temple of the Holy Ghost.

Jesus has taken my sicknesses and my diseases. No if, an, or butts, no matter what it looks like or how I feel, I know within my heart Jesus Christ has set me free from sicknesses and diseases. At the moment of this revelation great anger, yes great anger, rose up in my heart against the enemy of my Lord. The demonic world has no right to afflict me or any other believer, because Jesus took our sicknesses and bore our diseases.

Now I had been born with terrible physical infirmities, but now I found myself speaking aloud with authority to my ears, commanding them to be open and to be normal in the name of Jesus Christ of Nazareth. Then I spoke to my lungs and commanded them to be healed in the name of Jesus Christ of Nazareth. Next, I commanded my sinuses to be delivered, so I could smell normal scents in the name of Jesus Christ of Nazareth.

The minute I spoke the Word of God to my physical man, my ears popped completely open. Up to this moment I had a significant hearing loss, but now as I was listening to Christian music playing softly (at least I thought it was) the music became so loud that I had to turn it down. My lungs were clear, and I haven't experienced any lung congestion in 49 years. I used to be so allergic to dust that my mother had to work extra hard to keep our house dust-free. I would literally end up in an oxygen tent in the hospital. From that moment to now dust, allergies, mold, or any such thing have never come back to torment me or cause me problems. Instantly my sense of smell returned! I had broken my nose about four times due to fights, accidents, and rough activities. I could barely smell anything.

Suddenly, I could smell a terrible odor. I tried to find out where it was coming from and then I looked at

Vicki Jamison Peterson: God's Anointed Vessel

my feet and wondered if it could be them. I put my foot on a nightstand and bent over toward it. I took a big sniff and nearly fell over. Man did my feet stink! I went straight over to the bathroom and washed them in the sink.

The very 1st thing we must do to build a solid foundation for our lives is to let go of all our traditions, philosophies, doctrines, and experiences that contradict what is revealed to us through Jesus Christ. We must go back to Matthew, Mark, Luke and John rediscovering who Jesus Christ really is. Whatever Jesus said and did is what we agree with wholeheartedly. Any voice or teaching that contradicts Christ, and his redemptive work I immediately reject.

How God anointed Jesus of Nazareth with the Holy Ghost and with power: who went about doing good, and healing all that were oppressed of the devil; for God was with him (Acts 10:38).

The Circle Unbroken

My heart was quickened to gather with people of like-precious faith who loved Jesus Christ. I discovered a little full gospel church on our military base in Adak, Alaska, where I was stationed. When we began to worship the Lord in that little church, the Spirit of God would quicken within my heart. It felt like a fire in my belly rising up within me. Something wanted to come forth out of my mouth. I didn't realize it was the Spirit of God, so I tried to resist it.

As I resisted this unction of the Holy Spirit, I began to shake uncontrollably. People right around me in the pews gathered in a circle and laid their hands upon me. As they were praying for me, I broke forth and spoke out in tongues. When I did this, the interpretation of what I had said came out in English. I did not realize at the time that this is what the Bible calls the diversity of tongues and interpretation.

Wherefore let him that speaketh in an unknown tongue pray that he may interpret (1 Corinthians 14:13).

*God, Where Are You? This Little Teaching Could Save Your Life!

In our walk with God, there are many things that we absolutely must learn. I wish that we could instantly learn them - just from reading the Bible. But ... this is not the case. I had to learn a very hard lesson early in my Christian walk, one that many believers who have walked with God for years still have not learned.

I believe the reason that I had to learn this lesson was because of the amount of trials, tests, and hardships that I was to experience throughout my lifetime. I had to learn how to not live by feelings, or by the circumstances that surrounded me.

Vicki Jamison Peterson: God's Anointed Vessel

I gave my heart to Christ on February 18th, 1975

My whole life before this had been filled with pain, sorrow, depression, low self-esteem, physical disabilities, etc. You name it, I had it. But when I gave my heart to Christ, the presence of God instantly overwhelmed me. It was like electricity going through my body, twenty-four hours a day, seven days a week. This did not go away, but continued upon me.

I was instantly set free from all addictions, as well as emotional and mental problems. I was a brand-new creation in Christ Jesus. I fell in love with my Lord: head over heels. I immediately began devouring the Word of the Living God; specifically, the four Gospels. I got filled with the Holy Ghost, healed, and I preached my first sermon very shortly after I was saved. I think I took the presence and touch of God upon my life for granted, at that time, as if that was the normal, everyday experience, for every believer. I was soon to discover this was not true.

One morning I got up early to pray and read my Bible - as normal - but something was wrong. I had grown used to the very tangible presence and manifestation of God but, to my shock and horror, it was gone! I mean, to me, personally ... the presence of God was gone. Confusion suddenly clouded my heart and my mind. I cried out to God: "Lord, what's wrong? How have I offended you?"

I did not hear any answer, which was, to me, also very strange. The Lord was constantly speaking to my heart. I examined myself to see if there was something I was doing that was against the will of God.
I could not find anything wrong. I didn't know what else to do and I didn't really have anyone that I could go to, at that time, who was mature enough to help me.

So, I kept reading my Bible, kept on praying, worshipping, praising, and sharing Christ as I went along. I went to bed that night with no sense of God's presence. The next morning, I got up early, hoping that His presence had come back, but to my shock and sadness, God was not there. Once again, I went through the torment of examining my heart, crying out to Jesus and following my regular routine throughout the day. I went to bed that night in the same condition.

During the whole experience, I did not back off or give up but just kept pressing in.

This went on, day after day, after day. God just was not there in His tangible presence. Yes, I did get depressed, but I did not give up. I did not stop praying or reading my Bible. I never ceased worshiping and praising God. I did not stop sharing my faith with others and telling them the wonderful things Jesus had done for me. I think approximately two weeks went by with me in this spiritual desert —a no man's land— a dark and dry place in my daily walk.

Vicki Jamison Peterson: God's Anointed Vessel

I did not know what was wrong, and there was nothing else I could do but keep pressing in closer. After about two weeks, I went to bed one night, praying and talking to God, even though He was not answering me in the same way as He did before.

The next morning, I got up early and began to pray ... when out of the blue God's presence came rushing in stronger than ever - like a mighty wind.

It was like a powerful tsunami, a forceful flood of His presence and His Spirit. God's touch was upon me greatly. I began to laugh, to cry and to shout. Oh! It was so good to have God with me again.

I said to the Lord, when I was finally able to talk: "Lord, where were you?" There seemed to be a long pause, then He said to me, with what seemed to be a bit of amusement in His voice: **"I Was Here All Along."**

"You were, Lord?" **He replied: "Yes."** Then He said something that would forever change my life: **"I was teaching you how to live by faith."** He began to very specifically teach me out of the Scriptures, that man does not live by bread alone but by every word that comes out of the mouth of God.

Matthew 4:4 But he answered and said, It is written, Man shall not live by bread alone, but by every word that proceedeth out of the mouth of God.

I learned that our walk with Him does not depend upon our feelings, emotions, location, or circumstances. And that many of those who are believers are destroyed by the enemy because they do not understand nor believe this. Even the Apostle Paul had to learn how to be content in Christ, in whatever condition, trusting God, knowing that He is not a man that He should lie. Christ said that He would never leave us nor forsake us. We may call upon Christ with a sincere heart: knowing that He will be there for us, to answer us and show us great and mighty things which we know not!

Over forty years have come and gone since I learned this lesson. I now no longer allow the feelings of either His absence or His presence to affect me. Of course, I constantly examine my heart, but if I can find nothing wrong, I simply realize that I am flying by instruments and no longer operating by visual flight rules **(VFR)**. Thank God, as the aviation industry would say, I am SFR rated! There are two sets of regulations governing all aspects of civilian aircraft operations: the first is Instrument flight rules **(IFR)** and the second is visual flight rules **(VFR)** defined as flying by sight and sensory input. All Christians are to be rated as (SFR) which would equate to Spiritual Flight Rules!

MANS HERNIA HEALED

One night I was at a fellowship gathering with other believers from our little church. Chief officer Lloyd and his wife, Bonnie, had invited us all to come to their

Vicki Jamison Peterson: God's Anointed Vessel

house for fellowship. Now as I was standing in their front room enjoying the fellowship, a kind of foggy image came floating up from my heart into my mind. In this semi-foggy vision, I saw a bulge in the lower stomach area of the man standing directly across from me. I did not know that this bulge was actually what they call a hernia. I had only been born again for about a month, and not yet been taught on the gifts of the Holy Ghost. This was the word of knowledge operating by a vision inspired by the Holy Ghost.

As I saw this image in my mind's eye, I said to the Lord in my heart: Lord, if this image is really of you then let that brother come over to me. The very moment this little prayer left my heart, this navy chief (Frank) looked up and walked over me. I then also walked toward him, and we both reached out our hands towards each other, shaking hands. He introduced himself as Frank. As we were making small talk, I brought up the image I just had. He looked rather surprised and informed me that he was indeed having a terrible time with a hernia. The doctors had operated on it three times up to this point he informed me, but it had torn loose after each operation. I asked him if I could pray for him pertaining to this problem, and he gave me permission.

I told him that I would like him to put his hand over this hernia and that I would place my hand over his.

Then I simply prayed but not a long prayer. I simply spoke very quietly to this hernia telling it to go away in the name of Jesus Christ, and for his stomach muscles to be healed. The moment I finished praying, it disappeared.

The hernia was instantly and literally sucked back into his abdomen; it was gone! We both stood there, being wonderfully surprised, and rejoicing in the miracle that God had just performed. How this miracle came to pass is that God had given me "a word of knowledge and operating with the gift of faith and healing." Frank and I became good friends afterwards. At times we would go fishing out on the Bering Sea for halibut, but that's a whole another story.

For to one is given by the Spirit the word of wisdom; to another the word of knowledge by the same Spirit; to another faith by the same Spirit; to another the gifts of healing by the same Spirit (1 Corinthians 12:8-9).

Satanic Worshiper Delivered

My first encounter with a demon-possessed man was in 1975. I had only been a Christian for about two months, and I was in the Navy at the time. I was stationed on a military base on Adak, Alaska. One night (at about 8 p.m.) I was witnessing in my dormitory room to three men doing Bible study.

While sharing biblical truths with these three men, another man entered my room. We called him T.J. This individual had always been very different - and strange. He was kind of out there!

Vicki Jamison Peterson: God's Anointed Vessel

I had never even spoken to him, up to that time, except one night when he showed a nasty movie to the guys in his dorm. I had walked out of his room, not being able to handle his level of filth!

When T.J. entered my room, he took over my Bible study and began to preach some weird, off-the-wall things about the devil. He said he was from California where he had been part of a satanic church. He showed us the ends of his fingers in which some of the ends were missing from the first joint out. He told us that he had eaten them for power, and he had drunk human blood at satanic worship services. As he spoke, there seemed to be an invisible power speaking through him. An evil and demonic darkness descended upon us in my dormitory. A visible, demonic power took him over, right in front of our eyes, and his eyes filled with a malevolent glow! One of the guys in my room, Hussein, (who was a Muslim) declared this was too much for him, and left the room. The other two, Bobby and Willie, sat and listened.

I had never encountered anything as sinister and evil as this before. I honestly didn't know what to do (at that time) so I went downstairs to the barracks right below me. There was a fellow Christian I'd had the opportunity of working with, who lived right below me. After I had given my heart to Jesus Christ, Willie, the cowboy, told me that he too was a born again, Spirit-filled Christian. I had yet to see the evidence of this in Willie's life, but I didn't know where else to go. I went down to his room and knocked on Willie's door. When he opened the door, I explained to him what was happening in my room.

I was able to get him to go to my room. Willie stepped into my dormitory and stopped.

We both saw that T.J. was now up on a stool, made from a log, and he was preaching under the power of satanic spirits. At that very moment, cowboy Willie turned tail and ran out of my room. I went after him! He told me that he had no idea what to do and that he could not handle this. He left me standing outside my door alone.

I went back into my room and did the only thing I could do: I **Cried out to Jesus Christ**. The minute I cried out, looking up towards heaven, I'm telling you, a bright light from heaven shone right through my ceiling. It was a beam of light about three feet wide, an all-glistening bright light, shining upon me. I do not know if anyone else in my room saw the bright light. All I know is that the Spirit of God rose up within me, and I was overwhelmed with God's presence.

My mouth was instantly filled with an amazingly powerful and Prophetic Word from Heaven. I began to preach Jesus Christ by the Power of the Spirit! As I began to speak by the Spirit, the power of God fell in that room. The next thing I knew, T.J. had dropped to the floor, like a rock. T.J. began squirming just like a snake; his body bending and twisting in an impossible way. There was no fear left in my heart as I watched this demonic activity. There was nothing but a Holy Ghost boldness and divine inspiration flowing through me at that time.

During this divine encounter of Heaven, both Willie and Bobby had fallen on their knees, crying out to Jesus to save them. At the same time, they gave their hearts to the Lord, and they were both instantly filled with the Holy Ghost!

The next thing I knew, I found myself kneeling over the top of T.J. as he was squirming like a snake. I placed my hands upon him. Willie and Bobby came over and joined me, they also laid their hands upon T.J. With a voice of authority, inspired by the Spirit, I commanded the demons to come out of the man in the Name of Jesus Christ. As God is my witness, we all heard three to five different voices come screaming out of T.J.!

When the demons were gone, it was like T.J. breathed a last, long, breath, like that of a dying man, and he was completely still. After a while, he opened up his eyes - now filled with complete peace. At that very moment, he gave his heart to Jesus Christ. I led him into the baptism of the Holy Ghost. The presence of God overwhelmed all of us as we gave praise and thanks to the Lord. The next Sunday these three men went with me to church.

Evil Personified

T.J. the man I had cast the demons out of, came to my room one night. His heart was filled with great fear, because he had been so deeply involved in the satanic realm. He was hearing satanic voices telling him that they were going to kill him. One night as I was sleeping, T.J. began to scream. He was yelling that the devil was there to kill him! I sat up in my bunk and looked around. From the position of my bed, I saw the light of the moon shining through our big plate glass window. There, on our wall, was a shadow of a large, demonic entity. I was not making this up. This entity moved across the room towards T.J. The very atmosphere of the room was filled with a terrible presence of evil. Fear tried to rise within my heart, but the Spirit of God quickened courage and boldness within me.

I rose up out of my bed, commanded this demonic power to leave our room and never return in the name of Jesus Christ of Nazareth. The minute I spoke to it in the name of Jesus, I heard a screeching voice, like fingernails scraping across a chalk board. The shadow was pulled out of the room, as if a gigantic vacuum cleaner had been turned on, and it was being sucked up by an invisible force. This demonic power never came back again.

Behold, I give unto you power to tread on serpents and scorpions, and over all the power of the enemy: and nothing shall by any means hurt you (Luke 10:19).

When the unclean spirit is gone out of a man, he walketh through dry places, seeking rest, and findeth none. Then he saith, I will return into my house from

Vicki Jamison Peterson: God's Anointed Vessel

whence I came out; and when he is come, he findeth it empty, swept, and garnished. Then goeth he, and taketh with himself seven other spirits more wicked than himself, and they enter in and dwell there: and the last state of that man is worse than the first. Even so shall it be also unto this wicked generation (Matthew 12:43-45).

How to Live in the Miraculous!

This is a quick explanation of how to live and move in the realm of the miraculous. Seeing divine interventions of **God** is not something that just spontaneously happens because you have been born-again. There are certain biblical principles and truths that must be evident in your life. This is a very basic list of some of these truths and laws:

1. You must give **Jesus Christ** your whole heart. You cannot be lackadaisical in this endeavour. Being lukewarm in your walk with **God** is repulsive to the Lord. He wants 100% commitment. **Jesus** gave His all, now it is our turn to give our all. He loved us 100%. Now we must love Him 100%.

My son, give me thine heart, and let thine eyes observe my ways (Proverbs 23:26).

So then because thou art lukewarm, and neither cold nor hot, I will spew thee out of my mouth (Revelation 3:16).

2. There must be a complete agreement with **God's** Word. We must be in harmony with the Lord in our attitude, actions, thoughts, and deeds. Whatever the Word of **God** declares in the New Testament is what we wholeheartedly agree with.

Can two walk together, except they be agreed? (Amos 3:3).

For the eyes of the LORD run to and fro throughout the whole earth, to shew himself strong in the behalf of them whose heart is perfect toward him (2 Chronicles 16:9).

3. Obey and do the Word from the heart, from the simplest to the most complicated request or command. No matter what the Word says to do, do it! Here are some simple examples: Lift your hands in praise, in everything give thanks, forgive instantly, gather together with the saints, and give offerings to the Lord, and so on.

   I can of mine own self do nothing: as I hear, I judge: and my judgment is just; because I seek not mine own will, but the will of the Father which hath sent me (John 5:30).

Vicki Jamison Peterson: God's Anointed Vessel

4. Make **Jesus** the highest priority of your life. Everything you do, do not do it as unto men, but do it as unto **God**.

   If ye then be risen with Christ, seek those things which are above, where Christ sitteth on the right hand of God. Set your affection on things above, not on things on the earth (Colossians 3:1-2).

5. Die to self! The old man says, "My will be done!" The new man says, "**God's** will be done!"

   I am crucified with Christ: nevertheless I live; yet not I, but Christ liveth in me: and the life which I now live in the flesh I live by the faith of the Son of God, who loved me, and gave himself for me (Galatians 2:20).

   Now if we be dead with Christ, we believe that we shall also live with him (Romans 6:8).

6. Repent the minute you get out of **God's** will—no matter how minor, or small the sin may seem.

   (Revelation 3:19).

   As many as I love, I rebuke and chasten: be zealous therefore, and repent.

7. Take one step at a time. **God** will test you (not to do evil) to see if you will obey him. *Whatever He tells you*

to do: by His Word, by His Spirit, or within your conscience, do it. He will never tell you to do something contrary to His nature or His Word!

For whosoever shall do the will of my Father which is in heaven, the same is my brother, and sister, and mother (Matthew 12:50).

Then went he down, and dipped himself seven times in Jordan, according to the saying of the man of God: and his flesh came again like unto the flesh of a little child, and he was clean (2 Kings 5:14).

ABOUT THE AUTHOR

Dr. Michael and Kathleen Yeager have served as pastors/apostles, missionaries, evangelists, broadcasters, and authors for over four decades. Doc Yeager has authored over 380 books. They flow in the gifts of the Holy Spirit, teaching the Word of God with wonderful signs and miracles following in confirmation of God's Word. In 1982, they began Jesus is Lord Ministries International, Biglerville, PA 17307.

Vicki Jamison Peterson: God's Anointed Vessel

<u>Some of the Books Written by Doc Yeager:</u>

"Living in the Realm of the Miraculous 1"

"I need God Cause I'm Stupid"

"The Miracles of Smith Wigglesworth"

"How Faith Comes 28 WAYS"

"Horrors of Hell, Splendors of Heaven"

"The Coming Great Awakening"

"Sinners In The Hands of an Angry GOD", (modernized)

"Brain Parasite Epidemic"

"My JOURNEY To HELL" - illustrated for teenagers

"Divine Revelation Of Jesus Christ"

"My Daily Meditations"

"Holy Bible of JESUS CHRIST"

"War In The Heavenlies - (Chronicles of Micah)"

"Living in the Realm of the Miraculous 2"

"My Legal Rights To Witness"

"Why We (MUST) Gather!- 30 Biblical Reasons"

"My Incredible, Supernatural, Divine Experiences"

"Living in the Realm of the Miraculous 3"

"How GOD Leads & Guides! - 20 Ways"

"Weapons Of Our Warfare"

Dr Michael H Yeager

"How You Can Be Healed"

"To Many Books To Mention"

Made in the USA
Coppell, TX
08 May 2025

49136750R10118